9/11 SURVIVORS' STORIES

Midwest Memories

American Pride, Inc.

Dave Barso
WTC 1, 57th FLOOR

Copyright © 2021 American Pride, Inc.

All rights reserved. No part of this book may be reproduced or used in any manner whatsoever without the express written permission of the publisher, except for the use of brief quotations in a book review or other article or post featuring or discussing the book.

This is a work of creative nonfiction. The events, people, and conversations are portrayed to the best of the authors' and contributors' memories and recollections of experiences over time. While all the stories in this book are true, some names and identifying details have been changed to protect the privacy of the people involved. Any opinion or statement contained in the book is that of the identified author or contributor and not necessarily that of American Pride Inc.

ISBN: 9781737713203

CONTENTS

Title Page
Copyright
Foreword
Preface — 2
The World Trade Center — 10
1WTC, 57th Floor — 14
1WTC 59 - Laura — 26
1WTC 59 - Bridget — 43
2WTC 105th Floor — 60
WTC (Subway) — 72
WTC (Hotel) — 88
The Response in the Midwest — 99
The Pentagon — 104
Pentagon — 106
Intern at the Pentagon — 143
Ticket to a Memorial — 151
Union League Club of Chicago — 156
Willow House — 160
Acknowledgement — 174

FOREWORD

By Gary Sinise

We all tend to remember and know where we were, what we were doing and how we felt on 9/11/2001, as we learned of those horrific terrorist attacks in New York, Washington DC, and Shanksville, PA. I met several 9/11 Attack Survivors at the Union League Club of Chicago in 2005 at AT&T's Pentagon Memorial Fund Luncheon, which included one survivor sharing his account. It was powerful and moving to hear Ryan Yantis recall surviving the terrorist attack and the heroism that was on display on that awful day. The luncheon had been put together to raise money to build the 9/11 memorial at the Pentagon and I was donating my services and my band for a concert later that summer. Gary Sinise and the Lt Dan Band performed at the Pentagon Memorial Concert at Park West in Chicago, and that night other 9/11 Survivors shared their stories as well. In this book the Survivors continue and expand their efforts to help others learn what it was like to be there, and how luck, service, and sacrifice helped them to survive. Their unique, but shared, experiences expand their stories into a Midwestern perspective, adding different voices to the larger national narrative. I am glad they are sharing their stories with future generations.

Gary Sinise
Actor and founder of the Gary Sinise Foundation

Photo taken in 2005, Union League Club of Chicago

Don Bacso, US Marine Colonel, Gary Sinise, Laura Murphy, Ryan Yantis

PREFACE

by Ryan Yantis

When you are with friends and colleagues who shared the same life-altering event, there is comfort. And if you all have had time, support, and a mission to accomplish, a strong sense of community and belonging makes things easier. You don't have to elaborate or explain things like why certain sounds, smells, or memories cause asymmetric reactions. And, importantly, you don't have to open up and share your soul about one of the most impactful, emotional, and painful days--and periods--of your life. They just get it. They get you. You get them. There is understanding. There is comfort. That is what we had in the Pentagon, post-9/11 for the survivors.

But on a nice spring day in 2005, I was anything but comfortable. I was with friends, but I was very much alone. I found myself in an exceptionally large, fancy, wood-paneled Club of Chicago for a professional luncheon. There were 45 huge round tables, each seating ten, with amazing settings of white linen and shiny silverware; a very polite – and posh – experience. In the main dining room of the Union League Club of Chicago, approximately 450 business, civic, and social leaders, sat quietly after introduction and applause. As I was getting ready to speak, I swallowed hard. My Army service uniform – "the Greens" – was hot and felt very confining. Sweat was starting to trickle down my back.

Looking up from my notes on the podium, I saw the faces,

so many faces. Some were eager and leaning in; others were pensive, perhaps in anticipation for my Pentagon 9/11 survivor's story. At the table I had been sitting at moments before, were the club's president, selected leaders of Chicago's veteran community, AT&T executives, USO Chicago leaders, and actor Gary Sinise. It was so cool to be at lunch with Gary – I mean Lt. Dan! He is an amazing actor and a main character of the movie Forrest Gump – one of my favorite movies. He was going to speak after me.

Yikes! How had I gotten here? Why the hell was I in front of all these people, to share something I was not even comfortable in talking about? What the hell was I going to tell them about that day? Why was I not following the golden rule about not asking your audience to be your therapist? Gah!

And yet I knew why.

Months before, my wife and I had been guests at a black-tie event and we were seated at the AT&T table, at the request of the Chicago USO. As an advisor to the USO Board, as one of my additional duties, we enjoyed these social events and the opportunity to connect with business and social leaders in Chicago. Sharon Tyk, one of the dynamic executives from AT&T, was seated to my left, and she leaned in to talk to me.

"I need your help, Colonel," she said," I need to find a Pentagon 9/11 Survivor, ideally here in Chicago or somewhere in Illinois."

Already a couple of drinks into the evening, I remember replying that it should not be a problem. I guess I was a little too glib or flippant.

"No, really. I am serious. We – AT&T – are working on a project with artist Peter Max and we want to raise funds for the Pentagon Memorial Fund," she replied.

"You have one," I said, pointing at my Army Staff Badge,

which I wore with an unauthorized black mourning ribbon tied around it. "I am a Pentagon 9/11 Survivor. What do you need?"

In the years since, I should have relished this moment more, as it knocked her back on her heels a bit and left her a little speechless. Sharon Tyk is a power of nature and a dynamo. When she's working on a project or has a mission to accomplish, she's very impressive; active and energetic. She also can talk rapidly, conveying a mix of instructions, questions, observations, and orders, all in a polite and business-like manner.

She's told me since that she could not believe it was so easy to find a Pentagon 9/11 Attack Survivor. It had to be divine intervention, fate, kismet, or plain amazing luck. But then I remind her that she has to put up with me in the course of veteran events and activities.

In later meetings and discussions, AT&T with Sharon as the champion, we planned and developed a plan for fundraising in Chicago, featuring the 9/11 print by artist Peter Max, and a benefit concert with Gary Sinise's amazing musical group, the Lt. Dan Band. The weeks melted into months, and as the concert date approached, we wanted a good event to get the attention of the public in Chicago. We had decided on a launch luncheon at the Union League Club. I would speak, Gary would speak, and we would raise awareness for the concert and the art print, and maybe even get some other businesses and influential people as sponsors.

I remember my talk as being painful, hard to deliver, and a bit too long. I was wound up with too much raw energy and passion. I had issues I had yet to unpack and deal with. In every real sense, it was emotional, draining, and yet cathartic. I remember the pride I felt in talking about what I had seen others do and my memories of witnessing selfless acts of courage, compassion, and caring. A sense of shame for not having done more, for judging myself harshly against an unrealistic standard. My survivors' guilt, for having lived, when others paid a higher price in pain or the ultimate sacrifice, and for being on duty when my nation was attacked and impotent to do anything more to stop them, or to really fight back.

I recall blubbering and getting choked up and emotional in my remarks, and the relief I felt at the applause when I finished. Spent, I was back in my chair, recovering when Gary spoke.

He was awesome. He was everything I was not. Poised. Articulate. Brief. I remember being so impressed by Gary, and grateful he was stepping up as the new Bob Hope for the post-9/11 world, by helping the USO and entertaining troops. He and his band were going to play and bring music and happiness to people, and to help us raise money to fund and build the Pentagon Memorial.

Later that summer we held the concert at the Park West on Armitage Avenue, on the north side of the city. Gary and the Lt. Dan Band performed beautifully, with energy and style, in the beautiful, large, and private auditorium. I was so pleased we raised a great deal of money, and that World Trade Center survivors and other military, and veterans were able to be there. The event was a hit. In addition to raising awareness and funds, it also helped many of us heal and to feel more comfortable in our status as survivors. That meant a lot then, and still does today. It also helped me realize I needed to keep healing and to find more help for my survivors' guilt and other issues.

Survivor's Guilt And Being The Unicorn

When I moved out to Chicago, I left the environment of the Pentagon and the larger military community I had existed in since the attacks. Every day at the Pentagon was a reminder of that day, and the days, weeks and months since, but I was not alone. The great men and women I worked with had, by in large, had the same experiences I had, or theirs were close enough that we largely spoke the same unspoken language. We were survivors. We had processed our losses, and there was strength in numbers and the anonymity that comes from being one of the pack.

Being away from the Pentagon and in a new area where people were anxious to meet and learn more about the military, I was out on a limb, vulnerable and more than a little exposed. I was something of a "unicorn", a mystical, mythical being people wanted to see and talk to, to ask questions of, to debate half-baked conspiracy theories with, and to vent to. At times it was incredibly challenging. Fortunately for me, I had a chance encounter with a World Trade Center survivor, Joe Dittmar, who led me into contact with Willow House. Through Willow House, I found and helped shape a community of Survivors here in America's heartland.

It turned out there were a bunch of Chicagoland area World Trade Center survivors, all with amazing and heartbreaking accounts of what they faced that day, the choices they made, the nightmare and visions that haunted them. Professional men and women from multiple backgrounds and walks of life, we met and formed our own little VFW to share our stories, to open up about our feelings, and to process and unpack the burdens we all carried since Sept 11, 2001. What became a "typical meeting" for the survivors also became the bedrock for our public speaking efforts and this book as well.

By The Numbers

From the 9/11 Commission Report, Executive Summary, page 1 & 2

At 8:46 on the morning of September 11, 2001, the United States became a nation transformed.

An airliner traveling at hundreds of miles per hour and carrying some 10,000 gallons of jet fuel plowed into the North Tower of the World Trade Center in Lower Manhattan. At 9:03, a second airliner hit the South Tower. Fire and smoke billowed upward. Steel, glass, ash, and bodies fell below. The Twin Towers, where up to 50,000 people worked each day, both collapsed less than 90 minutes later.

At 9:37 that same morning, a third airliner slammed into the western face of the Pentagon. At 10:03, a fourth airliner crashed in a field in southern Pennsylvania. It had been aimed at the United States Capitol or the White House and was forced down by heroic passengers armed with the knowledge that America was under attack.

More than 2,600 people died at the World Trade Center; 125 died at the Pentagon; 256 died on the four planes. The death toll surpassed that at Pearl Harbor in December 1941.

This immeasurable pain was inflicted by 19 young Arabs acting at the behest of Islamist extremists headquartered in distant Afghanistan. Some had been in the United States for more than a year, mixing with the rest of the population. Though four had training as pilots, most were not well-educated. Most spoke English poorly, some hardly at all. In groups of four or five, carrying with them only small knives, box cutters, and cans of Mace or pepper spray, they had hijacked the four planes and turned them into deadly guided missiles."

9/11/01 is a date we will—and must—never forget. We all remember where we were, what we were doing, and how we felt as we learned of those horrific terrorist attacks in New York, Washington DC, and Shanksville, PA.

Nineteen terrorists hijacked four commercial transcontinental airliners carrying a total of 256 innocent men, women, and children, and using the planes as weapons, deliberately struck three targeted buildings, two in New York City and the Pentagon in Washington DC. Of the 256, there were 33 flight personnel on the four aircraft who perished either in the hijackings, or when the planes crashed. Hundreds died in the moments of impact of each of the aircraft into the World Trade Center buildings, the Pentagon, and at Shanksville.

In addition to the more than 6,000 who were injured and required medical attention on 9/11 there were a reported 2,977 people killed. While the majority of those killed were Americans, citizens from more than 90 countries were killed by the terrorists.

The elapsed time of the attacks - from the first impact of AA Flight 11 into WTC 1 at 8:46 am to the impact of UA Flight 93 into the field at Shanksville at 10:03 am is 77 minutes. By comparison, the most popular running time of a Hollywood movie is 101 minutes. In those 77 minutes our world changed.

From the 9/11 Commission Report, Executive Summary, page 14

The 9/11 Attacks cost (the terrorist and their supporters) somewhere between $400,000 and $500,000 to execute. The operatives spent more than $270,000 in the United States. Additional expenses included travel to obtain passports and visas, travel to the United States, expenses incurred by the plot leader and facilitators outside the United States, and expenses incurred by the people selected to be hijackers who ultimately did not participate.

From the 9/11 Commission Report, Executive Summary, page 26

We call on the American people to remember how we all felt on 9/11, to remember not only the unspeakable horror but how we came together as a nation—one nation. Unity of purpose and unity of effort are the way we will defeat this enemy and make America safer for our children and grandchildren.

We look forward to a national debate on the merits of what we have recommended, and we will participate vigorously in that debate.

We hope this book, our contributions, memories and experiences, help keep that discussion alive and moving forward.

Some of the accounts and information provided by the Survivors and others may be upsetting or startling to the reader, especially those written in the immediate aftermath of the 9/11 Attacks. Names have been changed to protect the privacy of others. We have sought to represent those who paid the ultimate price with great respect, and hope we achieved that goal.

THE WORLD TRADE CENTER

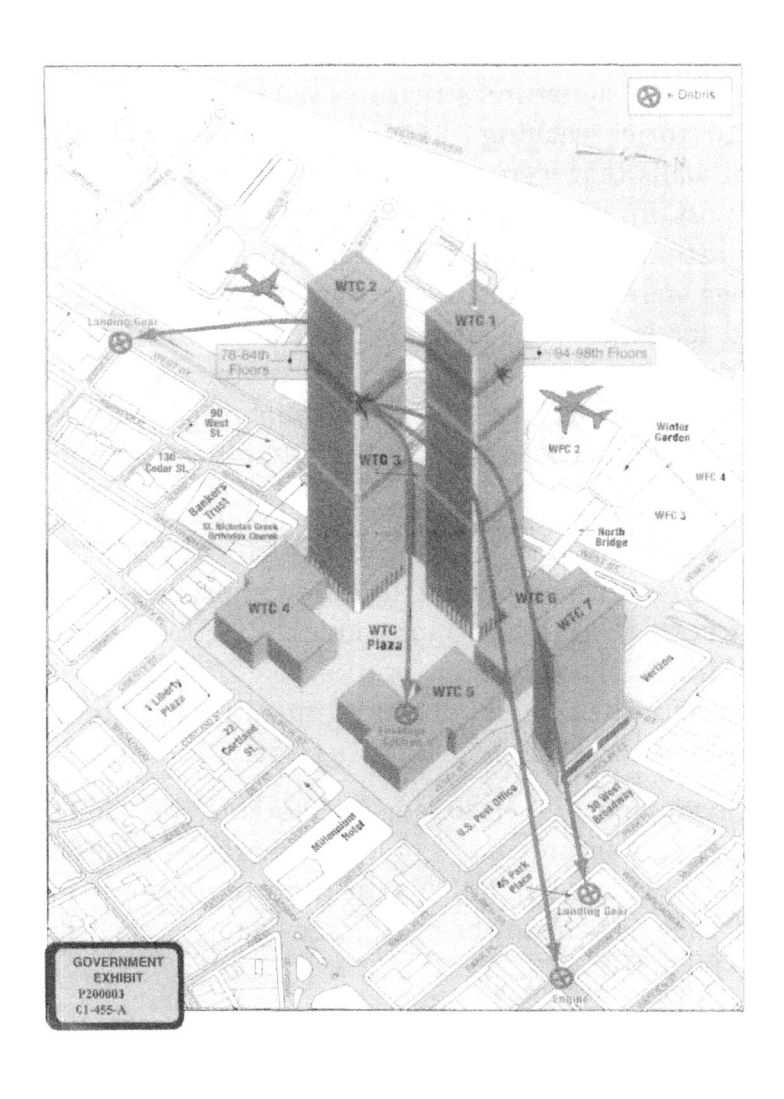

At the southern end of the borough of Manhattan in the Big Apple – New York City – the World Trade Center dominated the area and the skyline leading up to September 11, 2001.

The World Trade Center (WTC) complex was built for the Port Authority of New York and New Jersey, with construction starting in 1996. It was a dynamic and challenging build, eventually consisting of seven major buildings, and covering some 16 acres of high-value property in the financial heart of the City.

The two tallest buildings of the WTC complex were the "Twin Towers" of 1 WTC (North Tower) and 2 WTC (South Tower). These "signature" structures were nearly identical in design, 110 stories reaching 1,350 feet high. Both were square with exterior walls that were 208 feet in length. Each interior floor was almost one acre (43,264 sq feet) of space. The Twin Towers had more than 10 million square feet of interior office space. The buildings were constructed as a framed tube structure, which allowed for large open areas on each floor within the building, without interior weight-bearing walls or columns. They became, with their unique design a symbol of the culture of the United States and New York City. They dominated the skyline.

With more than 430 companies from 28 different countries, the World Trade Center was a focal point for the international finance, business, and trading companies. It is reported that on normal workdays approximately 50,000 people would be working in the buildings, with an addition 35,000-40,000 visitors. With the diverse concentration of thousands of people in the area, it also became a lucrative target for terrorists.

As previously mentioned, the World Trade Center buildings were very impressive, iconic landmarks of American and western power and strength. At the heart of the world financial district, they had already been attacked by terrorists before September 11, 2001.

But their fame and symbolism also made the Twin Towers

the targets of two terrorist attacks. The first took place on February 26, 1993. That day, a van loaded with approximately 1,200 pounds of explosives was driven into the public parking garage beneath the World Trade Center. The blast from the bomb created a crater several stories deep in the belowground levels of the complex and killed six people.

https://www.911memorial.org/learn/resources/digital-exhibitions/world-trade-center-history

The buildings in the World Trade Center complex included seven buildings, including one hotel and were connected with an underground mall known as the concourse. The Marriott World Trade Center was a 22-story, 825-room hotel operating at 3 World Trade Center at the southwest corner of the World Trade Center complex. Roughly equidistant between the Towers but to the northeast was the Plaza, a center for art and performance.

In the massive Twin Towers, there were hundreds of businesses, offices, agencies and spaces, some utilitarian, and other quite sleek and posh.

More than $100 million worth of art was destroyed on 9/11. An extensive collection of Rodin sculptures and drawings owned by brokerage firm Cantor Fitzgerald was lost. Works by Picasso, Roy Lichtenstein and Le Corbusier that belonged to companies with offices or businesses in the buildings were reduced to ash.

NY Post, https://nypost.com/2011/09/15/more-than-100m-in-art-lost-in-911-attacks/

In the massive piles of rubble, after the Attack, searchers sifted and looked for lost art, mostly in vain. The incredible heat and compression of the Towers as they collapsed destroyed everything. Plus, there were remains to be found, so families could finally know the true toll of 9/11.

NIST could not determine how many occupants were in the

path of the aircraft as it entered the tower. Those in the direct collision path were almost certainly killed instantly. Many more would have lost their lives from the burst of heat from the burning jet fuel. Fatal injuries were reported on floors as low as the Concourse Level, where a fireball swept through the lobby.

At 8:52 a.m., the first of at least 111 people was observed falling from the (WTC 1) building.*

The only thing that slowed or stopped the 9/11 Attacks were the actions by the FAA to clear the skies of all planes, and the actions such as those taken by the passengers and remaining crew of United 93, who tried to regain control of the aircraft from the terrorist. This amazing accomplishment of quickly and safely landing some 4,500 commercial, passenger, and private aircraft in a very short period of time saved lives and potentially disrupted other terrorist hijack team preparing to strike.

References:

The 9/11 Commission Report

https://www.9-11commission.gov/report/911Report.pdf

* Final Report on the Collapse of the World Trade Center Towers; National Institute of Standards and Technology, Sept 2005

https://nvlpubs.nist.gov/nistpubs/Legacy/NCSTAR/ncstar1.pdf

1WTC, 57TH FLOOR

by Don Bacso

From a very young age, I was always taught to work hard, do well in school, and get a college education to better yourself as an adult. This advice was passed down to me from my parents. Even though my parents divorced when I was only five years old, they both emphasized a hard work ethic. My father was a laboratory technician for a large petroleum company and my mother worked as a bookkeeper. The divorce left me and my three siblings in a quandary; my mother didn't make that much money in her career and needed to provide food and shelter for her children. There were many times that my mother sat at the kitchen table crying, wondering if she should pay the bills or buy food for us. It was a constant struggle for her, and many times we were left with eating peanut butter and jelly sandwiches or buttered noodles.

From my experiences as a youngster, I was later able to motivate and push myself toward my goal of achieving a college degree. I walked across the stage in May 1993, to receive my Bachelor of Science degree in business from Purdue University. My first position out of college was working as the technical services manager for a non-profit organization, which provided a good salary and benefits for my wife and me. However, I was looking to expand my experiences and achieve more for myself in my career. In 1997, I began my consulting position for a small firm in Chicago, then started with a new consulting firm on September 11, 2000. There, I expanded my professional expertise in migrating companies from one email system to Microsoft Exchange email, travelling throughout the United States for several such projects. As a senior consultant, it was not unusual for me to be in New York one week, Washington D.C. the next, and Houston the week after that; travelling was part of this job.

As my one-year anniversary with the company approached, I planned to take a golfing vacation with some friends in Myrtle Beach, South Carolina. I had already purchased my plane ticket and put a deposit down on a hotel room. However, as the planned vacation got closer, my boss said that he needed me to go to New York for a one-week business trip from September 10th to 14th. I knew I had to go and, unfortunately, had to cancel my planned vacation to Myrtle Beach.

The trip to New York was a familiar one to me; I had flown out of Midway Airport and landed at LaGuardia on a few occasions already. On one business trip, my colleagues and I were treated to a Yankees game in the Bronx. I was in awe to watch a baseball game in the "House that Ruth Built". On my prior business trips to New York City, I had stayed at the Millenium Hilton or World Trade Center Marriott, as they were the closest in proximity to World Trade Center (WTC) Tower 1, where I was conducting my email migration. Since I had made a few previous trips to the WTC, I became familiar with the buildings and their surroundings. I knew where to find the security desk, where all the best food places were located, and the best shops for souvenirs. I had paid close attention to where stairwells and elevators were located in case of an emergency, as well.

Now, it is time for me to take you on a personal journey of tragedy and triumph. This is my personal recollection of the events before, during and after September 11, 2001. At the time, I lived in Dyer, Indiana. It's a small Indiana town on the border of Illinois, about 35 miles south of Chicago, that was a great town to put down roots and raise a family. My wife and I had one son at the time, and she was five months pregnant with my second son.

I guess that I should start a few days before that fateful trip with a specific, but ironic, comment made to one of my parents. It was September 9th, and I was attending my nephew's birthday party. Near the end of the party, I made the comment to my father that I was flying to New York the next day for a week-long business trip. I also mentioned that I was going to be in One World Trade Center, the one bombed in 1993. My father was concerned about this fact. After assuring him that security in that building was extremely tight since the first attack, I made a comment that would come back to me, so ironically, on 9/11. "Don't worry Dad, lightening never strikes the same place twice."

I flew to New York from Chicago on a crisp, clear Monday morning. It was the first flight out of Midway that morning and the plane was completely full. I was in an aisle seat only five rows from the cockpit. I made myself comfortable in my seat while a person in my row was already sleeping against the window. During the flight, I noticed something that would later be so chilling; the flight attendants were able to go in and out of the cockpit very freely with no lock and a thin door. I thought to myself at the time, "Anyone could just walk right into the cockpit if they wanted too, and that can't be too safe. The flight was approximately 90 minutes and gave me time to work or get in a quick nap; I slumbered off to sleep until the descent into New York.

Upon arriving, I took a cab from LaGuardia Airport to my hotel in Manhattan, five blocks from the WTC. I actually asked to stay closer, as I had on two previous business trips, either at the Millenium Hotel, across from the Center, or in the World Trade Center Marriott, located between the Towers. Again, as fate had it, both hotels were fully booked, and I would have to stay at the hotel five blocks away.

After checking in, I began the walk to the WTC. I remember seeing the Towers as I rounded the corner, and only one word could describe them--magnificent. As I had experienced before, they were a bustling metropolis of business activity. During any given day, in the afternoon, there could be approximately 50,000 people in the Twin Towers or subsidiary buildings. On a few previous occasions, while walking into the WTC in the morning, I felt like a fish fighting to get upstream. Droves of citizens were exiting the bowels of the WTC subway station and walking to their final destinations. There was a vast diversity of cultures and languages spoken in the WTC complex. While walking into the building, I could overhear conversations in French, Indian and Chinese.

Once I arrived at 1 WTC, I went to the 59th floor to meet with my colleagues from the New York office. In addition, two women from my Chicago office were also there, Laura Murphy and Bridget Pakowski. After spending about a half-day at work, some of my colleagues from the New York office wanted to have dinner. We all decided to eat at a small Italian restaurant in the shadow of 2 WTC. It was raining slightly that night, but sitting below the Towers, in that restaurant, was awe inspiring. Around 8:00 p.m., I told everyone good night and I would see them in the morning. I had mentioned to most of those colleagues that I would be going in early on Tuesday morning to get a jump on some work.

Tuesday, September 11th, 2001, was my one-year anniversary with the consulting firm and it was beginning as a beautiful, warm day. At 7:45 a.m. that morning, I arrived at 1WTC to begin my workday on the 57th floor. Usually, when I'm working in a remote city or location, I don't get to work until 9:00 or 9:30 a.m., knowing I could be working late into the evening. For some unusual reason, I decided to go in early that fateful day. I was working alone in an interior computer server room; on the floor, rows and rows of servers, hummed along. I turned on my laptop to begin loading software for my project and noticed through online messaging that Laura and Bridget were working on the 59th floor.

At 8:46 a.m., there was a large "THUMP", followed by a huge, drawn-out explosion. The floor in the room lifted me up and put me back down. The rows of servers shook and shuddered, the monitors went off, then immediately back on. "WHAT THE HECK IS THIS?" I was thinking. Then, the building began to sway violently to the south, then back to straight, and then north again. It was at this point I thought, "BOMB", and the building is beginning to collapse. I was scared and thinking, "I am going to go down with this building." After swaying violently back and forth a few times, the building came back to center and settled. I regained my composure—somewhat--and balance while on my feet. All I could think of was, "I need to get out of here, where is the closest stairwell?" As I exited the server room, I could hear the metal beams creaking within the walls, due to the stresses put on them from the swaying.

Upon exiting the server room, I found four strangers in the hallway from the New York office. I said to them, "What the heck was that?" No one knew; I just got blank stares. Then, from a corner office, an attorney yelled, "Come here, look at this!" From his window, we pressed ourselves against the glass and could see the dark smoke and flaming debris above us. Paper was raining down from the upper floors and it looked like a ticker tape parade had started. At this point, I thought we had been hit by something a few floors above us. It was not unusual to see multiple helicopters or small planes flying around Manhattan on a daily basis; could one of those have accidently hit us? The ground below, in the plaza, was littered with debris. I asked the four people, "Where is the closest stairwell, this can all wait for another time." They all agreed, and we headed for a stairwell. We all hustled pretty quickly to the stairwell entrance, but there was no panic. We were going to start walking down 57 floors of stairs! That did not even enter my mind until I thought about it well later that day.

When we got to the stairwell, maybe five minutes had passed since the impact, but the stairwell was already packed with people coming down from the floors above. The people coming down were very calm and helpful to others. Conversations in the stairwell ranged from, "What happened" to, "We were hit by a commercial jet plane." How could we get hit by a commercial jet on such a clear, beautiful day? It must have been a medical emergency on the plane or something like that. Yes, that had to be the only explanation to what had happened.

It was a very slow process, going down a flight of concrete stairs, waiting for more people to enter the stairwell, going down another flight of concrete stairs, and then waiting for more people to enter the stairwell. I was down approximately five to ten floors, when at 9:03 a.m., there was a muffled concussion, and the stairwell shook for a few seconds. People began screaming and crying, and I thought, "Is this our building, is the building coming down on us?" At that point, everyone stopped walking and waited for something to happen. Nothing happened, someone a couple steps up behind me yells, "GO!", and all the people begin to walk again. I had no formal evacuation instructions, nor had I experienced any fire drills in that building; I just went down the stairs in hope of getting out and seeing my family again.

During the slow process of descent, the crowd would yell from above, "Move right, injured coming down!", and that was the first time I saw how badly burned some people were. With the assistance of other good Samaritans, a woman, then a man walked down the stairs. Their arms were in front of them, wanting no one to touch them; they were severely burned on their arms and backs. I immediately noticed the smells, particularly the smell of jet fuel. Why jet fuel? Did anyone else smell jet fuel?

Around the 44th floor, the smoke began to rise up in the stairwell. It was thick, gray smoke and I couldn't even make out people two floors below. I put my shirt sleeve over my nose to filter the air better. People were not panicking at this point, but I could see concern in some people's faces. I thought, "Now what? I can't continue down this stairwell with all the smoke." So, I opened the door on 44, which is a switchover for elevator banks. Right then, a security officer asked, "Is that stairwell filling with smoke?" I stated it was, and he began hustling people to another stairwell that was clear of smoke to the bottom. At first, I was apprehensive about leaving the security of that first stairwell, but I knew I could not possibly make it to the bottom with all the smoke rising up. That gentleman was a savior for myself and the many that followed me to the other stairwell.

After approximately 35 to 40 minutes in the stairwell, I reached the ground level of the building. We could not cross the plaza because of all the debris littering the ground and the unsafe conditions, so we were hustled down an escalator and through a mall below the World Trade Center Plaza. The overhead sprinkler system was on, and we were told to run and not use our cell phones. Everyone around me remained calm and my nerves felt considerably better seeing NYFD and NYPD personnel escorting people out of the plaza. Once we were able to come out of the underground mall, about a block away, I was able to turn around for the first time and see the Towers. The upper third of 1 WTC was rolling with thick, black smoke. The upper half of 2 WTC was engulfed with thick, black smoke. Thousands of pieces of debris littered the ground, for over a block away.

I was at Church and Vesey Streets. With the adrenaline still pumping through me, I knew I had to get to my hotel, or at least a phone to tell my family I was alive. I started to walk east, away from the Towers, down the middle of Vesey Street, toward my hotel. I could see the expressions of numerous people's faces looking at the Towers; I knew what was happening behind me, but I did not want to see it. I was no more than a block from the WTC. when I heard my name being called out, "Don, Don!" I turned around and ran into Laura Murphy and Bridget Pakowski, who were in the Tower that morning from the Chicago office. We grabbed each other and hugged, and I told them we should get back to my hotel to make phone calls. We could see voice messages adding up on our phones, but we could not make any outgoing calls.

It took us approximately five to ten minutes to walk back to my hotel on William Street. When we made it there, we were inside no more than five minutes, when the ground began to shake. At first, we didn't know what caused the shaking. From the TV in the lobby of the hotel, it was Tower Two collapsing. The sky went light gray, gray, then black for at least a minute. People who had been watching the events unfold at Ground Zero were now diving into my hotel to get out of the dust and debris cloud. Remarkably, very little dust and debris made it into the hotel during the collapse. Approximately 30 minutes later, the whole scenario would repeat itself as Tower One collapsed. Laura, Bridget, and I were in my room when the second tower imploded. I remember saying to them to hold on to something, because I did not know which way the tower would collapse.

We finally found public phones on the second floor of the hotel. I was conferenced into my home from the Chicago office, and my wife, Jennifer, answered the phone. "Hello," she said. I said, "I am alive, I am okay." Then, I broke down in sobs. After the call, and assuring her I was fine, I went to a corner of the room to get the rest of my emotions out.

After our phone calls, the ladies and I watched the news coverage of the attacks from my room. We then knew the true extent of the attacks across the East Coast. After a short period of time, the water was shut off to my room; I can only assume this was to have more water pressure down at Ground Zero, to assist in fighting the fires. Since we didn't have running water, the ladies made the decision to start walking north out of the Ground Zero area to an office location in Midtown Manhattan. It took us close to an hour of walking and taking a cab, but we did make it to our central office location. We all were exhausted at this point, and our coworkers made us feel so good with offers of food and drink.

It was around 2:00 p.m. on September 12th when I was able to get a Ford Taurus rental car with Laura and Bridget. This car was brand new with low miles and I was looking forward to driving it back to the Midwest. However, what I would discover shortly into our trip, was that the car had no cruise control; oh, my aching right calf muscle!

I decided to drive the first leg of the trip. We saw very few cars on FDR Drive in Manhattan and when we approached the George Washington Bridge to enter New Jersey, we could see incoming traffic was halted at the New Jersey state line.

We drove on I-80 straight through, 14 hours, to get back to our families. We only stopped for the necessities: food, gas, bathroom breaks. All gas stations were open, but not many people were on the road during our trip. My wife kept calling me during the drive home; "Where are you?" she would ask. "I will be home soon, get some sleep," I answered. It was September 13th, around 4:00 a.m. when I pulled up in front of my house. My wife met me outside. I grabbed her, cried and said, "I never thought that I would see you again." My mother was in town, staying with my wife at our house that week. I grabbed her; she was crying and said, "You're not traveling anymore for business, are you?" I said "No, not at all. I will be staying close to home from now on." I was exhausted, I could not sleep that night, and my mind was racing.

Over the next few days, family and friends came over to see me. It felt very good and helped with the healing process. I had nightmares during the first month or so; those have since subsided. It was too emotional to watch anything about the Towers on the television.

```
NAVIGANT INTL SIDLEY              CLIENT: BACSO/DON
ONE FIRST NATL PLAZA 39TH FL             01
CHICAGO                 IL    312 357-8662   INVOICE: 7295330    PAGE:01

20 SEP      UNITED            FLIGHT:  696   CLASS:  V
  TH        CHICAGO/OHARE     DEPART:  700A
            NYC/LAGUARDIA     ARRIVE:  959A

20 SEP      MARRIOTT TRADE CENTE      MARRIOTT          212 938-9100
  TH        3 WORLD TRADE CENTER NEW YORK NY 10048
            IN: 20SEP OUT: 24SEP  CONFO: 82285509

24 SEP      UNITED            FLIGHT:  677   CLASS:  Q
  MO        NYC/LAGUARDIA     DEPART:  500P
            CHICAGO/OHARE     ARRIVE:  641P

**NOTE**TICKET VALID ON UNITED AIRLINES ONLY**           TICKET: 0167092813266
```

Itinerary for scheduled return trip to NY on September 20, 2001

In the weeks following 9/11, I had so many emotions going through my mind. I was angry, sad and guilty. I was angry at the people who could do this to innocent citizens on such a beautiful day. I was sad for the thousands of families that no longer would have a father, mother, brother, sister, aunt, uncle or child; yes, there were children on those planes. I felt guilty because I was still here. Why was I spared when so many innocent people perished?

At the same time, I felt so very proud of my fellow Americans and their show of patriotism after September 11th; the American flag being flown on cars, trucks, houses, you name it. I'm also so proud of the bravery, the police and firefighters, the ones in New York, who I owe my life to, and the ones around the country. When you see one of them, give them a pat on the back or a handshake, and tell them how much they are appreciated; I don't think they hear it as much as they should. They are truly

American Heroes. I was grateful in the weeks after 9/11 to meet many of the first responders in my, and surrounding, towns. The police and firefighters took me under their wing and allowed me to talk about whatever was bothering me. To this day, I remain a friend to many of them and would do anything in support of these everyday heroes.

A few years after 9/11, I was able to meet many survivors from the Midwest through a support organization called Willow House. For about a year, the survivors were able to meet and discuss, laugh and cry about the challenges that faced each of us. I am forever grateful for this group and Willow House for getting me through the most difficult event in my lifetime.

After confronting the issues, I faced on that fateful day, I decided it was to time to give back to the community that supported me for so many years. What better way to support my community than by giving my time to its youth? I decided to run for the school board and served proudly for 12 years ending in 2020. This was not only a very satisfying endeavor but it gave me the opportunity to meet and garner friendships with so many individuals committed to public education of our youth. I am very proud of the accomplishments while serving on this school board.

Beginning with the first anniversary of 9/11, I began to speak at various events about my experience on that day. I have spoken every year on the anniversary, to remind citizens to never forget that day. It is never easy to speak about that day, but I must continue to tell the story of the incredible heroism and sacrifice, so that the heroes of that day will not be forgotten. We as a nation need to stay vigilant and not be complacent as we do not need another repeat of September 11, 2001.

1WTC 59 - LAURA

by Laura Murphy

In 2001, I was a project manager for a Chicago-based technology consulting firm, leading a portion of a larger team made up of external consultants and client staff. Our team had spent the previous few months getting to know each other and planning for a desktop upgrade for a multi-office law firm based in Chicago. The firm had recently merged with a New York-based firm, and they were moving its Midtown office to the World Trade Center (WTC).

Our project in New York was to set up new PCs for the Midtown staff to use once they moved to WTC in a few weeks. Bridget was the firm's project manager, who was also in Chicago. We had been out to WTC in August for planning meetings and flew in on September 10th to do staging.

I had first been to New York City (NYC) in the early 90s for a spring break trip with other theatre department classmates, and we had a great time going to shows and exploring Soho, Midtown and Times Square. Since then, I had been back to NYC on various business trips for an array of law firm clients. Some trips allowed for reconnecting with old friends, while other trips had me working until the wee hours of the morning to ensure VIP PCs were ready for big business mere minutes after I released them. I hoped this staging trip might allow for some sight-seeing and visiting.

On the evening of September 11, 2001, I spoke with my mother by telephone. She suggested that I write everything down as it happened, right away, while it was all fresh. Most of what you read here is from my recounting that Tuesday evening, 20 years ago.

First, a note about my account. My companions and I are not heroes, just folks who, by the grace of God, survived this terrible ordeal. I have found that telling this story, letting people connect with someone who made it out somehow makes them feel a little better. It is difficult to comprehend the growing number of missing and our hearts breaking to see the folks on the streets of New York desperately seeking loved ones. One person from the firm remains on the missing list (later confirmed to have died when the second tower fell).

Second, we did, on our journey, crack wise a time or ten. My advanced apologies if you are offended at the casualness of some of our comments. Surely the situation was dire, depressing, and desperate. However, each stage of the journey was the focus of the moment and finding little things to laugh at was the alternative to becoming overwhelmed by the sheer force of events we were in the middle of. I hope you will understand.

***

As I start to write this it is now 12:02 am, actually September 12, about 17 hours after the first plane struck WTC Tower 1, the North Tower. That's the building we were in.

Yesterday, Bridget and I checked into the Millenium Hilton, across the street from WTC and got to work.

Welcome

Name: HARIL, LAURA
Room No. 4307

Hilton

Millenium Hilton
Next to the World Trade Center

55 Church Street
New York, NY 10007
www.newyorkmillenium.hilton.com
Phone (212) 693-2001 · Fax (212) 571-2316
Toll-Free Reservations 1-877-692-4458
or 1-800-HILTONS

Guest Service Hotline
Touch 6100

If there is anything at all we can do to make your stay more comfortable, simply touch the button marked "Guest Service Hotline" on your guestroom phone or dial the extension above.

Check-Out Time: 12:00 p.m.

This morning, Bridget and I are on the 59th floor, having

arrived around 8:00 a.m. We have just gotten some breakfast and are sitting in conference room 59P, wondering where our setup has gone from the day before. We went to Ken's office to see if we could get longer cables than what we had come up with so far.

While we're standing in his office doorway, the building begins to sway and shake. Ken just looks at me and keeps saying "oh, my God," over and over. Bridget and I stay in the doorway, my hand gripping her shoulder; I don't want her to move out of the doorframe. "Earthquake!" I think for a second, but then think we are too high for some reason, in New York. Later, I wonder what we might have seen if we'd been in the conference room at the time. We had unboxed and stacked several dozen desktop computers in a room down the hall and I heard them clatter to the ground. I think, well that's going to be a problem, this is going to put us behind, and we haven't even started.

When the swaying stops, Ken says, "I have to get to my station."; he is a floor monitor-type guy. Bridget and I run back to the conference room to grab our stuff, because instinct dictates that you can't just leave your stuff. (Of course, you *should* just leave your stuff; this is how people die, staying in their routines in the beginning of a crisis.). I look out the window and see papers, hundreds of papers, whirling in the air outside and call her attention to it.

Flinging laptops and other essentials into our bags, we're in the stairwell in less than two minutes, passing Ken who is directing all to the stairs. As we begin to descend 59 floors, the air is clear and folks are calm; a few older, heavier-set women must stop, their legs are shaky, still, they are calm and will resume the trek. The stairwell easily accommodates two people walking side by side and that's how Bridget and I descend. Early on a man is going up; "no, no one goes up!" we say. "I need my stuff," he says. "LEAVE IT!" we shout--easy for me to say, I have my stuff, leaving only a sweater behind. Later, one man is stranded in a wheelchair, some men from the building are with him and they are calling for assistance on their walkie-talkies. There is some chatter, fairly calm, but no one around us knows what has happened. Many of the people in the stairwell were here eight years ago, when the parking structure under WTC had been bombed, so they knew the routine: get down, get out, get to safety.

We must stop a few times; firemen, many of them probably killed in the collapse, pass us going up, humping up dozens of flights of stairs with equipment--God bless them and their families. "Move to the right!" We do and pass the word up the stairs.

The air is clearer as we go lower. Between what I saw out the conference room window, the air getting cleaner, and talk from folks in floors above us, we know that whatever happened, happened above us. There's water on the stairs as we get lower; I worry about us all slipping and falling, creating a domino effect. But we move on safely; spirits are good, breathing is good. My pager is going off and my cell phone is getting messages, but I can't listen. I know it's my mother, I know she's worried. She's one of the only people who knew exactly where I was going to be; since I have a cell phone, I don't widely publicize my whereabouts. The lights go out and come back on and we have to stop occasionally. Of all folks, it's some burly dudes that start to freak out a little; another man tells them to chill, and they do. We exit the stairs, directed to keep moving. A chunk of ceiling tile falls and hits me in the head, no damage, skull's way too thick!

We're walking through on the concourse level of WTC 1 and see that the elevator signs are akimbo. "Don't look out the window," a Port Authority officer says, so of course I do. There's a burning chunk of something metal in the plaza. (I realize later it's part of a plane, probably the second plane which struck WTC 2 while we were in the stairway. We didn't notice that impact in the stairs; maybe it was the time the lights flashed off for a second.) They send us down the escalators through the mall.

There's broken glass, the sprinkler systems are raining smelly brown water down on us. I pull out my umbrella; a man looks at me and we smile at the silliness of that. Finding little somethings to laugh at keeps us from freaking out. As we come up the escalator, we are hurried out of the building by NYPD and PA officers – New York's FINEST. We go out to cross Church Street, hearing them say, "Keep moving, do not look up." Of course, I look up. "I've just walked down 59 flights of stairs," I say aloud, "I want to know what's going on!" I turn and look, stunned at what I see. I can only see one tower, with burning, black, dark thick smoke trailing off into the sky. We won't know until later what has happened.

We make our way across and down the street and see that the Millenium Hilton, where Bridget and I are staying, is cordoned off. I don't look up at it; I just tuck away the thought in my mind that we aren't going back in there.

We are over by the church now, just standing there, looking back at the Towers. They are both still standing and there are many people walking away from the site. We don't really have anywhere to go, what with our hotel closed and not a very good sense of where we are in relation to anything else. The authorities have been focused on getting everyone out and away from the buildings. Now, a block or so away, we're on our own. I'm sure all the people who commute to WTC are trying to find a way to get home, but some are possibly looking for coworkers, friends, family.

Suddenly, among the thousands streaming out of both buildings, Bridget sees Don, another person working on the rollout, who I'm just meeting now for the first time. He had been on the 57th floor and came down a different stairwell. He saw some more challenging things on his walk down, we learn, as we hook up and head towards his hotel, the Club Quarters. It's a fine irony, considering Bridget and I didn't want to stay there because it's so far from the WTC and sometimes we work very late.

We get to the hotel and walk into the TV area. Now, for the first time, I see what has happened, the planes slamming into WTC 1 and 2, as well as the Pentagon. Obviously, terrorism, I am instantly filled with rage and anger, just like everyone else. But I let it go; there's still too much to do, to focus on. Anger and grief, those can come later. Now is about moving from moment to moment, focusing on the next task at hand. Right now, that task is getting word out that we are okay.

We head up to Don's room on the 21st floor. We can't get a line out on the phone and the front desk tells us to try the pay phones on the second floor. We are heading there when, unknown to us, Tower 2 collapses. I can feel the vibration of the shockwave come through the building as I am leaning up against the wall, waiting for the elevator. Before we can get a line out, an announcement comes over the PA, instructing everyone to go to the first floor. We get down there and see lots of "Pillsbury Doughboys", folks caught in the debris from the collapse. The hotel staff help them out, wiping them off, giving them water, towels, etc. Eventually, we get back up to the second floor and desperately try to reach someone in Chicago to let them know we are okay. It seems to take forever, maybe really just 30 minutes or so. Finally, we get through to the voicemail of Joy at my client. Bridget, Don, and I leave numbers of folks to call. We are feeling better. I call Joy "the facilitator" and I know our messages are in good hands.

We go back up to Don's room because the hotel folks tell us that the air is better in the rooms. We are watching the news when Tower 1, our building, collapses. We watch out the window of this room on the 21st floor, about eight blocks from ground zero. Within 30 seconds, the debris field hits, first white, then gray, then black--black for at least 30 seconds. We are all still anxious. Finally, a text page comes into my pager. It's from Phil, a co-worker back in Chicago. It says, "Glad to hear you are OK. We are contacting your family." A great cheer for Phil goes up and the tension comes down another notch. Our families and friends will soon know we are okay.

After some time, during which we scout the vending machines for a few bags of snacks (the remainder of which is later embedded in the bottom of my laptop bag, attracting my dogs to the Chips-Ahoy-scented plastic), the phone lines in the hotel rooms are working again. We make phone calls; I get in contact with family, Don and Bridget do the same. Okay, now what? So far, each moment since the first strike has been filled with doing the next thing. I am restless staying in the hotel, so we scan our options. Not knowing Manhattan, we're trying to figure out just how far away things are; they look really far.

We debate staying. I'm concerned about the area becoming dangerous at night. Then, the water is cut off because they need the water and pressure to fight the fires. So, we decide to leave. Figuring out where to go is another story. All our options-my company's NY office, a co-worker's apartment, the client's other office-all are miles away and (we figure) accessible only by walking. Finally, we decide to head to the client's other office at 53rd and 3rd Avenues. Looking outside, every surface is covered with a half-inch to an inch of soot and papers and the air is still pretty thick with dust. We put wet towels on over our mouths to help with breathing. It's about 3:00 pm.

A few blocks into our journey, Bridget's shoe breaks. We joke that had she known there was going to be a bombing she would have worn more sensible shoes. (My slides stay together for the duration and years later were still in my closet, with the dust from the fallen Towers embedded in between the woven leather.) She has the sense to think of getting socks out of Don's suitcase and wears those the rest of the trip. She quickly wins the "best dressed refugee" award of the trio.

We walk through the debris, heading northwest to pick up Broadway for our trip uptown. We pass the site; it is difficult not to stop and stare. I try to be respectful of what Don and Bridget were experiencing as they stand there, staring at the hole, but I have to yell at them to keep moving. We must keep moving, not knowing the real time and distance of our journey nor the condition our world will be in as we venture north.

We had felt, back in the hotel, that all of Manhattan was in the same condition as our area and felt trapped by debris and dust and chaos. At one point, looking out the window, I remembered reading *The Stand* by Stephen King, and how frightening the description of dystopian Manhattan was, especially the tunnels. That's what I was most afraid of encountering, just vast swaths of what we were looking at. Once past the site though, a few blocks north, there is no debris, the air is clear, and we drop our nose cloths. We walk on amid a most amazing thing--no traffic in Manhattan; now, that is bizarre. Way down on Broadway, we find an open drug store and buy some essentials, toiletries and the like. Yeah, we bought underwear. Hey, what are you laughing at?

We walk on and finally get a cab around 29th Street. Many cabs had driven on, saying they were going home. That made me mad; my feet hurt, I was tired, and I didn't want to walk any more. Finally, a cab picks us up. We mention how hard it has been to get a cab. He tells us that all the Arab and Arab-American cab drivers are going home because they are being assaulted, physically and verbally. I notice then that he is Asian. The cabbies that had not picked us up, I realize in retrospect, had at least looked as though they could be from the Middle East. I am sad and disappointed, angered and ashamed of the stupidity of some of my fellow Americans.

The cabbie drops us at the Midtown office, at 53rd and 3rd Avenues; it's about 5:30 p.m. now. The office has tables covered in food--deli trays, cookies, a spread to feed an army--and people, finally a feeling somewhat of safety. I have myself a little cry. We check email and vmail. I find it amusing to see the emails within my company that say, "Laura is heading to our NY office" (I share a laugh with my Chicago officemates the next week, saying, "I have no idea where the NY office is!"). We relax a little, decompress. They try to find us lodging for the night, but all the hotels in the area are booked up by this time. One of the guys that works there, Tony, offers to put us up at his apartment, not too far away. A woman, Migna, goes on a search to find Bridget some shoes. I comment that I think red would do nicely. Of course, Migna comes through with red, and gray, and black--a whole bag of shoes.

Bridget, Don and I leave the office building with Tony, Migna and Tom. Their favorite watering hole is still open, so we go in there. Watching TV, President Bush comes on. I stare at the TV, wanting to jump through the screen and get a big hug; George, make the bad man go away. He assures me he will. When he begins to recite the 23rd Psalm, I am overcome, put my head down and cry for a moment, then return to watching. I am comforted by his words, by the Word.

The six of us stay at Tony's tonight, the girls claiming the bedroom, and we stay up late into the night, talking. Bridget wants to know why we survived. We catch a few hours of sleep.

The next morning, Tony has gone out early and picked up food – real food – omelets, hash browns, toast, and coffee; fabulous and very thoughtful. We hop on the phones and, after a while, track down a rental car. We watch TV while we wait to leave.

Later, we say goodbye to our friends and catch a cab over to the rental car place. We are waiting in a huge, long line. At one point, we look over across a parking lot and see people open a rental car office we thought was closed. One of us runs across to them and nabs third in line. We get a one-way setup, hitting the road at about 3:00 p.m. Talk about no traffic! We cruise up the FDR to the GW Bridge and head over into New Jersey. The traffic is thick heading back into Manhattan, with dump trucks, busses, some cars, and the National Guard. Going under a bridge, we look back to see a huge, beautiful American Flag, draped so that folks going into the city can see it. We really do have a great looking flag.

We stop at a mall in New Jersey to get some comfy clothes for the long drive. I have the worst hamburger of my life, but the cheese fries are good, and I really don't care. Once we're on I80, we just keep driving west. Believe it or not, the drive home is the scariest part of our journey to me. Don and I switch off driving as Bridget is, by her own admission, not much of a driver. I'm pretty good on the flat lands of Illinois but the hills of Pennsylvania at sunset with the sun in my eyes is about all my nerves can take--it was honestly the most harrowing part of the entire journey for me. After that, I think Don ends up doing about two-thirds of the driving. I drive across Ohio, nice and flat, just like Illinois. We listen to the news on the radio the entire drive. My friend calls me every few hours to make sure I'm awake, but I can't sleep even when I'm not driving.

We drop Don off at his house on the Illinois/Indiana border. His little dog comes running out of the house, such a cutie! His wife is, of course, glad to see him. Then I drop off Bridget in Cal City. Her dad is so nice and gets in his car and lead me back to the highway. Normally, I'd find my way, but it's about 4:00 a.m., and my brain is mush. I get to my mom's house about 5:00 a.m. and hug the fur off my dogs. It is good to be home. And alive.

The next day, Mom and I drop off the car at the rental place. I walk in and the lady behind the counter says, "Are you Laura?" It's Kathy, a girl I went to high school with; God's hand even in which rental agency we ended up with! She's one of the first to hear my tale, and I begin to realize that folks need to hear from people who have made it out, see them in person. It's good for me too, I'm sure.

The following Tuesday, I'm back at work. We have to rethink our project and how to move it forward. In late September, I fly to San Francisco, then on to Los Angeles to see my dad, then to Kansas City, the following week, following Presidential orders to get back in the sky and "get back to normal." I'm more uneasy with being away from home for any extended period of time right now than with flying or tall buildings. Others feel differently. All of it is understandable; you didn't need to be in the WTC or New York to be affected by this, for the attack was on America.

In retrospect, as I think about what the terrorists have done, we can see how well planned it all was. But God's plan is greater and never thwarted. Even God's plan for me on that day, as I look back, I see how clearly He moved us from place to place, connecting us with Don, getting us out of harm's way before the buildings collapsed, moving us uptown before the other buildings fell, finding us shelter for the night, getting us a rental car and seeing us home safely though we were exhausted from the journey, and sparing Bridget and I the horrific sights that will haunt the dreams of others for some time to come.

The world, as we know it, is different than it was just a few short weeks ago. Our country is at war. Someone asked me how I feel about sending in ground troops. How should I feel? I have many friends, loved ones, folks I care about who could end up in the middle of this. I find the prospect daunting, sad. It's been a long time since we had to fight a long, hard, tough battle.

And yet, freedom has never been free. There has always been a price and that price is most often human blood. 2,000 years ago, it was the blood of Christ that bought us our freedom from sin and death. We must seek the Lord's guidance during these times and always. We need to feel a sense of control over our lives. When chaos abounds, it is difficult to feel safe and protected, feeling instead that we have lost control, that evil has won the day. But the simple fact of the matter is that we are not in control, nor is evil. God is in control. That does not mean that He condoned or made this evil, cowardly act occur. On the contrary. I cannot explain the ways of God, nor is any man qualified to question His authority for He is infinite, and we are finite. But

God is clear in His Word that He has a plan, a big one for the world and a small one for each of us. Those who survived did so because of the grace of God; but that applies to each of us every moment of every day. We continue here on this earth because of His grace, His will. We continue because He is not done with us. It is not our job to question His will, it is our job to seek and do His will.

After I got home, I was reading Psalm 23, when I looked over and started reading Psalm 25. I found it to be very fitting, very comforting, and so, in parting, I share part of it with you.

Psalm 25

A Psalm of David.
To You, O LORD, I lift up my soul.
O my God, I trust in You;
Let me not be ashamed;
Let not my enemies triumph over me.
Indeed, let no one who waits on You be ashamed;
Let those be ashamed who deal
treacherously without cause.
Show me Your ways, O LORD;
Teach me Your paths.
Lead me in Your truth and teach me,
For You are the God of my salvation;
On You I wait all the day.

Remember, O LORD, Your tender mercies
and Your loving kindnesses,
For they are from of old.
Do not remember the sins of my
youth, nor my transgressions;
According to Your mercy remember me,
For Your goodness' sake, O LORD.

Good and upright is the LORD;
Therefore He teaches sinners in the way.

The humble He guides in justice,
And the humble He teaches His way.
All the paths of the LORD are mercy and truth,
To such as keep His covenant and His testimonies.
For Your name's sake, O LORD,
Pardon my iniquity, for it is great.

Who is the man that fears the LORD?
Him shall He teach in the way He chooses.
He himself shall dwell in prosperity,
And his descendants shall inherit the earth.
The secret of the LORD is with those who fear Him,
And He will show them His covenant.
My eyes are ever toward the LORD,
For He shall pluck my feet out of the net.

Epilogue

I have returned to Manhattan many times since 9/11. In February 2002, I went back to collect my things from the Millennium Hilton. Looters had gone through the hotel in the days following the attacks and took anything of value, using sledgehammers to break through walls, open doors and get into rooms. Considering the instability of the entire area, I was amazed at their brazen stupidity. During this trip, I went to the platform that was built around the perimeter of the site, Ground Zero. It was all raw plywood and there were so many messages scrawled of sorrow, desperation, loss, anger, vengeance, faith, prayers, and healing.

WTC:00
Viewing Platform
Broadway & Fulton Street

Admit One
Non Transferable
Not for Sale

Please DO NOT arrive more than 15 minutes prior.

Friday
February
22

Viewing
9:00-9:30 am

NYC & COMPANY

In early 2005, I returned to Manhattan for another client, but the project fell through, and I decided I'd had enough flying for a living. I think I stayed with traveling long enough to prove to myself I could do it. Suddenly, it didn't matter.

Twenty years on, I still live in the suburbs of Chicago. I'm married to a wonderful man, we had a beautiful daughter in September 2011, and I always have two dogs to keep me anchored on both sides. God is good and all-knowing, but not all-knowable.

I've never returned to the WTC site since 2002, never gone to the memorial. Maybe, some day.

AMERICAN PRIDE INC.

Patriot Day, 2004

By the President of the United States of America

A Proclamation

Three years ago, our country was ruthlessly attacked, and more than 3,000 innocent people lost their lives. We will always remember the victims: sons and daughters, husbands and wives, dads and moms, family members, co-workers, and friends. And we will always be inspired by the heroism and decency of our fellow citizens on that day: Police, firefighters, emergency rescue personnel, doctors, nurses and many others risked their own lives to save the lives of their fellow citizens. They demonstrated the great character and bravery of our Nation, and they embody the great spirit of America.

Since September 11th, America has fought a relentless war on terror around the world. We are staying on the offensive in this war—striking the terrorists abroad so we do not have to face them here at home. We pray that God watch over our brave men and women in uniform and all who are waging this war and working to keep America safe. And we pray for their families. In the face of danger, America is showing its character. Three years after the attack on our country, Americans remain strong and resolute, patient in a just cause, and confident of the victory to come.

By a joint resolution approved December 18, 2001 (Public Law 107-89), the Congress has designated September 11 of each year as "Patriot Day."

NOW, THEREFORE, I, GEORGE W. BUSH, President of the United States of America, do hereby proclaim September 11, 2004, as Patriot Day. I call upon the Governors of the United States and the Commonwealth of Puerto Rico, as well as appropriate officials of all units of government, to direct that the flag be flown at half-staff on Patriot Day. I call upon the people of the United States to observe Patriot Day with appropriate ceremonies and activities, including remembrance services, to display the flag at half staff from their homes on that day, and to observe a moment of silence beginning at 8:46 a.m. eastern daylight time to honor the innocent victims who lost their lives as a result of the terrorist attacks of September 11, 2001.

IN WITNESS WHEREOF, I have hereunto set my hand this tenth day of September, in the year of our Lord two thousand four, and of the Independence of the United States of America the two hundred and twenty-ninth.

George W. Bush

THE WHITE HOUSE
WASHINGTON

October 27, 2004

Mrs. Laura Bartl
Brookfield, Illinois

Dear Mrs. Bartl:

Thank you for your letter and kind words. I appreciate your taking the time to share your experiences on September 11, 2001.

In the time since that day, we have seen the character of our country in the resolve and compassion of the American people. The United States will continue to advance freedom to build a safer world and a more hopeful America.

Laura joins me in sending our best wishes. May God bless you, and may God continue to bless America.

Sincerely,

George W. Bush

1WTC 59 - BRIDGET

by Bridget Pakowski

When I think about September 11th, I always think about the time leading up to that day and the events that lead to some of us to be there from the Chicago office. My career with Sidley started as a college intern when I was just 19 years old. I originally joined because I wanted to go to law school and was so excited to have an internship at such a prestigious firm. I loved my job so much, that for the second semester of my freshman year, I changed my course schedule so I could work at Sidley on Mondays, Wednesdays and Fridays, cramming all my classes into Tuesdays and Thursdays. Little did I know that I would join and be loaned out to the IT department, and that would change my whole thinking about my future career goals. I did everything learning from the ground up, training, help desk and then eventually project management.

By 2001, I was already there almost 10 years, mostly part-time while I finished undergrad and, eventually, grad school. After I completed my master's degree, I was asked to come back to Sidley to help lead the project management teams & PMO. I was helping to lead the project team responsible for a unified image across the newly merged Sidley Austin Brown & Wood. Our plan was by October 1st, there would be a single image and unified systems, meaning they would have the same email, same document management and other systems to ensure the firm felt like one team. In order to meet this deadline, we planned a test of the new system for the week of September 10th.

From a personal perspective I was in my twenties and having the time of my life. Two weeks before the planned test, I was getting ready to take a flight to Dublin, Ireland, so I could attend the U2 concert at Slaine Castle on August 25th. The funny thing about that trip was that I was planning to fly out Thursday night, attend the concert on Saturday, and then fly back to Chicago on Monday. Looking back, that sounds insane, but I was young and carefree and not the least bit concerned about jetting off to Ireland and then to New York City soon after. I was travelling so much in those days, that I often said I used my driver's license to get on planes rather than to drive a car. I think it also shows a little bit why my parents were not 100% sure I was in NYC on the 11th since I was traveling a lot.

The Thursday morning of my flight to Dublin, I was at the office with my travel bag. My manager told me that I should plan to be in NYC early, because we were having some technical problems; she suggested I fly there Monday. I had to confess that I could probably get to the New York office on Tuesday but would have to fly directly from Dublin. Another minor problem was that I hadn't packed any work clothes. I couldn't very well wear my "Sox Suck" T-shirt to the office, for example, which I brought because my best friend and I were Chicago Cubs fans, and my other friend was a White Sox fan. The Cross-Town Classic (Sox vs. Cubs) had just happened the week before and we thought those shirts were really funny. Since I did not have enough time to hike back up to my apartment on Belmont from the Sidley office on State Street, I figured I would buy some work clothes when I got to New York.

I had an amazing time at Slaine Castle, despite the fact that it was very rainy, and the grounds were full of mud, and I did manage to get myself to NYC. I stayed at the Millenium hotel, as I always did, and upon arriving, I went to the underground shopping area and bought some professional clothes. Since it was still technically summer, I also bought a pair of black semi-professional wedge sandals. After working in that office for a few days, I headed home for Labor Day.

```
NAVIGANT INTL SIDLEY              CLIENT: PAKOWSKI/BRIDGET
ONE FIRST NATL PLAZA 39TH FL              01
CHICAGO                IL         312 357-8662    INVOICE: 7995515      PAGE:01

10 SEP      ATA                   FLIGHT: 272    CLASS: Q
   MO       CHICAGO/MDWAY         DEPART: 720A
            NEWARK                ARRIVE: 1045A

10 SEP      HILTON MILLENIUM              HILTON              212 693-2001
   MO       55 CHURCH STREET NEW YORK NY 10007 UNITED STATES
            IN: 10SEP  OUT: 14SEP  CONFO: 3136370207N

14 SEP      ATA                   FLIGHT: 277    CLASS: Q
   FR       NEWARK                DEPART: 300P
            CHICAGO/MDWAY         ARRIVE: 440P

NO CAR REQUESTED                                  TICKET: 3667094148398
YOU WILL NEED A PHOTO ID AT CHECK-IN.             FARE:         USD209.50
```

    I flew back to NYC on September 10th with Laura, joining our fellow Midwestern coworkers, Don and Damon. Our Chicago team had already formed a tight bond with the New York team; in the truest sense of a merger, we were operating as one project team. As soon as we arrived, we popped into the office, but, more importantly, we met for drinks at the end of the day at one of the many bars and restaurants at the World Trade Center (WTC). Even those who had to catch commuter trains to get home popped into say hi that night. Afterwards, the Chicago team headed back to their hotels. Most of us were at the Millenium Hotel. I remember Don had to stay at the Club Quarters, which was a few blocks away. We made fun of that at that time, not knowing it was going to be our saving grace the next day.

It's strange the things you remember, especially the little details. That next morning, September 11th, I woke up early and was starving. I put on this cute grey suit, and I chose a black t-shirt rather than a more formal top because it was so warm and we were planning to set-up the project "war room", which meant crawling around and putting in cables to build out the dedicated space to work (I'm grateful for Wi-Fi today). I also wore the black wedges I bought the week before. Laura and I headed to the office, stopping first at the WTC cafeteria. I grabbed water, Diet Coke and a sausage-and-egg on a hard roll, which was such a NYC breakfast and a novel concept for me at the time, since I was not a New Yorker. Our war room was the corner conference room on the 59th floor in the North Tower; our dedicated work home for the next several weeks. The view was amazing up there, especially on such a sunny day with beautiful blue skies.

As we ate our breakfast and started to get set up, we realized we needed more network cables and went looking for Ken, the network guy. We were standing at his office door when we felt the building sway and shake; I remember thinking was that an earthquake? Ken, who also happened to be the safety floor person, simply grabbed his vest and whistle and told Laura and I to head to the nearest stairwell. Instead of doing so, we instinctively headed back to the war room to get our belongings. Laura took off running down the hall; I remember running behind her, watching her legs as she ran in a long skirt with these backless flats. Clip clop, clip clop. When we got back to the room, we looked out the window; there were papers floating in the air, just sort of hanging there. We grabbed our bags and I remember looking at my laptop and my giant Diet Coke and left both of those behind, which ended up being a blessing because laptops were so giant at that time. Luckily, I did grab the bottle of water and we headed to the stairwell for our journey down. I would later be so grateful that we took the two minutes to grab our bags, rather than go down the first stairwell on the opposite side of the building, which would have been on the side of the impact.

Wearing my cute black wedges, I began clip-clopping down 59 stories. I remember the people on the stairs: there was a man who was there for his second day of work; there was a woman who had also been there in 1993 for the car bombing; and there was a man who was running up the stairs in the opposite direction, ignoring people as they told him to turnaround. We just kept walking round and round as we slowly made our journey down. The door would open on various floors and more folks would join the quiet descent. I remember my cell phone clicking, signaling messages were coming in but, with no service, I could not see who was calling. With all my travelling, I wasn't really sure who knew I was actually in NYC, let alone the WTC. My parents knew and I could only imagine their panic. As we got further down the stairs, that's when it got a little smokey. The lights flickered and went out and there was water in the stairwell. What was most heartbreaking was when people started calling out "on the left", which meant to move over as the firefighters were climbing up the stairs with all of their gear on, not knowing what was yet to come.

About forty minutes after entering the stairwell, we reached the bottom. The stairs opened to the ground floor lobby, which led to the underground mall area. There was a man there telling everyone to move and to not look out the windows, which, of course, you did. I'm not sure I can ever really explain what I saw, just metal and fire and smoke; it was like an apocalyptic sci-fi wasteland and the image is frozen in my mind. As we made our way through the underground mall area—the one I had shopped in just a few weeks earlier--the sprinklers were on, so Laura opened her umbrella. A guard paused to yell at us and then just smiled and waved us through, probably the first sign of gallows humor that came about that day.

When we climbed the stairs that led us to Church Street, it was a bit like coming out of a tunnel. The sun was still out, but there was debris everywhere. We still didn't know what had really happened at this point, thinking maybe there was a bomb or an earthquake. We had no idea that a plane had hit the North Tower, and certainly no idea that a second plane had hit the South Tower. We walked into a sea of thousands of people and police and fire fighters, surrounded by lots of noise and panic, sirens, lines and chaos. I think our first thought was to find a payphone, since we had no cell service. As we headed that way, I saw our coworker, Don, talking to a police officer. I started screaming, "Don" and headed towards him. I must have grabbed Laura and she went with me. I am not sure how we saw him through the chaos but, thank God we did. It was such a relief in this sea of humanity and chaos to see a familiar face; I still can visualize him standing there in a beige shirt.

None of us knew what was going on and the pay phone lines were really long, so we decided to head to his hotel a few blocks away. I think we walked in the street; there were no cars, except maybe emergency vehicles, but people were everywhere and frantic. Thank God we chose to go to the hotel, because just as we were entering the Club Quarters (CQ), the first tower fell. As we looked at the TVs in the lobby, there was a massive cloud of smoke and dirt and debris and everything that just came through the streets. The staff handed out cloth napkins, and I noticed then how dusty we were. I remember blowing my nose and there was debris from all the dust we inhaled.

There were several pay phones in the lower level of the hotel, where we tried to call our families, with no success; we either got busy signals or silence. Finally, I called the Sidley messaging 800 number and got through. I remembered Nick's extension, so I was able to direct dial him in our Chicago office. Thankfully, he answered. I let him know that we were ok and asked him to let the Chicago and Mid-town offices know. Then, I asked him if he could conference in our various family members. We didn't want to lose the connection, so I asked Nick to stay on for each individual call. I can only imagine the thoughts and emotions he was going through as he listened to me tearfully call my parents, or Don call his pregnant wife, or Laura call her family. We'll always be super grateful to him, as who knows when we would have been able to reach our family directly.

We then went up to Don's room to try to come up with a plan. The TV was on, and we watched that horrific image over and over again. I felt utter shock; it was so surreal that we were just in the middle of what everyone was seeing on TV, especially the fact that we were so well insulated as to what happened when we were living it. We only knew to evacuate; even when we were on the street, we were focused on figuring out where we were going. It took a while for the magnitude of the tragedy to sink in. Then, the news said the second building was falling. We sat on the floor, away from the windows, and watched in horror as the day turned dark and this wave of brown dirt went pass the windows with papers floating and a whoosh noise along with a little bit of earth shaking and rumbling.

After that happened, we strategized about just camping

out in Don's room for the night. Since we didn't know if another building was going to fall, we weighed the risk of staying put or going back out there. The room was a safe haven, and we decided to stay. We went to the hotel vending machine to get supplies; I remember getting Diet Coke and something chocolate. As the morning went to afternoon the city's mayor said they were shutting down water and power. People were to get out of lower Manhattan so the emergency workers could concentrate on the rescue. I think we were scared to leave--at least, I was scared to leave—but, it was more terrifying to think about staying the night without power or water during an active recovery. So, Don packed up his suitcase and we left to head uptown, after having to ask the front desk how to actually get uptown, since none of us was from New York.

As we started the four or five-mile walk, I remember the smell in the air; it was dusty, rancid, and smokey, with all these papers just blowing around. More gallows humor emerged when I kept saying, "hey there goes my project plan." It was eerily quiet in the city, except for the sirens in the background. We maybe only walked about 15 minutes, when my super-cute wedges finally broke. The top of them just came off and there was no way to repair them. That's when Don offered to carry me, which was very sweet, but not possible with the distance we were going. Instead, I put on a pair of Don's socks, and we kept walking. It was strange to walk in socks, especially because there was debris everywhere and I had to be careful not to step on anything.

At some point in the journey, the air started to clear a bit; I think we were in the Chelsea neighborhood by then. There were people out and walking about, not sure where they were going. We started looking for any store that was open, as I needed flip fops and Laura and I would need overnight supplies, like toothbrushes, etc. A few of the bodegas were open and we finally stopped and found the supplies we needed at a Rite Aid.

When we finally made it to the Sidley office, on 57th and

3rd Avenues, the first people I remember seeing were Migna, Tom, and Tony. I had worked at the Sidley office before, during other projects and team meetings. In fact, my first trip to that office was really my first trip to NYC, right after I graduated college. I felt really cool going there and staying at the Plaza. During that time, I had developed a strong bond with the people in the office; we had gone to Yankees' games, Broadway plays, dinners, and drinks, and even their homes. The Sidley NYC group were special people and as soon as we saw each other, we just all hugged and cried. Don, Laura, and I were so grateful we made it there; we didn't have any family in town, the only family we had were our Sidley co-workers. The only place we knew to go was the Sidley office. After the adrenaline-filled walk, it was a relief to be there, and I began to relax a bit. We saw that people were gathered in one of the conference rooms, trying to account for each of the employees that could have been in the Towers that day. They also fielded from family members, just as Joy, from the Chicago Sidley office, had when my mom called for news about me.

For a while, we just sat there, numb, until it was decided that we would stay at Tony's place for the night and figure out a plan from there. The sun was going down as we went, so it must have been around 5:00 or 6:00 p.m., and we first headed to a bar with some of the Sidley people. The power was out, so the bar was just giving out drinks and we really need them. The beautiful spirit of the New Yorkers came through that night. Growing up in the Midwest, I had always heard that New Yorkers were rude or fast-paced, but what I found out by working in New York--and even more profoundly on September 11th--was the amazing spirit, resiliency and generosity of the NYC spirit. At some point, Migna gave me a pair of red shoes, and someone gave me a T-shirt. Instead of going home to their own family or friends, they huddled with their work colleagues from Chicago.

Later that night, six of us crammed into Tony's one-bedroom apartment. I remember sitting on the kitchen floor, when survivor's guilt first started to kick in. Why was I alive when so many others had lost their life that day? Laura answered that question, "God is not finished with you yet." I barely slept that night, and that question of why did He allow me to survive would haunt me for years.

The next day, we somehow managed to get a rental car and Don, Laura, and I headed home with Don's luggage and the last set of Brown & Wood back-up tapes from the Mid-Town office. As all of the email and computer servers were destroyed when the Towers collapsed, these back-up tapes were the last record of the emails, documents and other files. When they reached the Chicago office, the team would bring them up and start the process of migrating to the new systems and ensuring the Brown & Wood team had their files and messages.

It was a long 15 to 16-hour drive home and everyone's nerves were fried. Don and Laura did most of the driving, while I was in charge of directions. Our first stop was in Pennsylvania, to grab food and buy some new clothes. I bought undergarments, sweatpants, a t-shirt, a burgundy cardigan, and some tennis shoes; I don't think I ever wore those clothes again. Once we got through the mountains of Pennsylvania and entered Indiana, it was a much smoother go of it. We dropped Don off first and then Laura drove me to my parents' house. I'll never forget seeing them sitting on the front porch in the dark, waiting for me. They were hugging me and crying and then hugged Laura. I would spend the next week at their house, recovering and crying, and trying to figure out what to do next.

I think staying at my parents' house and sleeping in my childhood bed helped me get through those early days. Sidley required me to talk to someone before they would let me return to work. At some point, one of my colleagues came to pick up the back-up tapes so the dedicated team could get the NYC office and people back to work. The firm strongly discouraged me from going to help in NY, as we had so many people there already.

Many articles talked about the leadership of Sidley Austin Brown and Wood and how they were able to get the office and their people up and running within days. It's strange to reflect now, that as we were heading west to go home, our colleagues from the Chicago and D.C. offices were packing U-Hauls with equipment and jumping in cars headed to NYC. They knew that the hundreds of employees who were located in the Towers had to learn how to use Exchange email and iManage; the objective of my project happened immediately.

Welcome home party 9/25/01
Bridget Pakowski, Liza Madden, Damon Wilkonson, Laura Murphy

After two weeks, I returned to work by flying to San Francisco. The Brown & Wood office there had moved to the new systems overnight like everyone else and needed help getting up and running. I think going there was so important to me because it was my small way of contributing to getting things back to "normal".

For the next few years, I travelled around the world, running projects for Sidley. There was a team of six to seven of us, who went to every single office, including San Francisco, Los Angeles, Washington, D.C., London, Hong Kong, Singapore, to name a few. These people became part of my family during the project. During this time, I knew that I was still being impacted and trying to process the events of 9/11 and some of those big scary questions, especially, "why am I here, when others lost their lives that day?" I often said that I lost several years of my life, just constantly running and making myself so busy traveling, running projects for work and partying with friends around the world. Of course, like anything in life, you cannot outrun yourself; eventually, you have to face it.

There were triggers that reminded me of the day. One of the biggest was the Northeast Blackout in August 2003. I had moved to the River North area of Chicago and lived in a high rise. When I saw that blackout happen across Ohio to New York I was paralyzed with fear. Was this another attack? Would this be coming to Chicago? At that moment, I decided I would need to leave Chicago and eventually relocated to Austin, Texas. There, I would meet my future husband and begin to find some peace.

For me, the journey to come to terms with what happened was a combination of time and solo work on my end. I think I finally started facing it when I moved to Austin in 2004. Being in another city, with close friends helped. I also took up running, which eventually led me to run the New York Marathon in 2011. Having dedicated time to focus on myself and some thinking time was a good combination. In 2008, I went to a solo retreat in Sedona, Arizona, which helped me release some of the hold from that day as well. Sedona is already such a high energy place and doing yoga on the Red Rocks, breath therapy and hiking helped me release the anger, fear, guilt, and other feelings that I held on to for so long.

AMERICAN PRIDE INC.

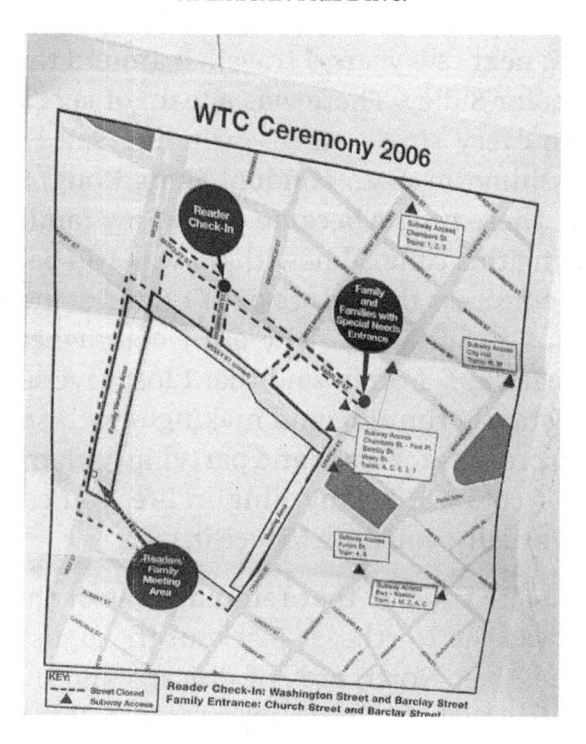

> FIFTH ANNIVERSRY
> SEPTEMBER 11TH
> COMMEMORATION
>
> 8:30 A.M.
> WORLD TRADE CENTER SITE
>
> PLEASE ENTER AT
> CHURCH AND BARCLAY STREETS
> BEGINNING AT 7:00 A.M.
>
> THIS INVITATION SERVES AS
> YOUR CREDENTIAL
> FOR ADMISSION.

One thing that helped me find some peace came in 2006, when a few of us attended the five-year memorial service. Living in Austin, I asked two of my best friends, Kristina, and Mary Jean, to come with me for moral support. My friends and I actually spent the night at the Millenium the night before the service. Don and Rohit, my friends, and coworkers, came with us as well. It was a somber day and we felt very emotional standing there for hours, watching the names being read out one by one and hearing the sobs from the families. It was so raw; the grounds were gated and dusty, the area was still a ghost town, and what it truly was is a massive grave site.

After the ceremony, we met other former colleagues at a local bar and caught up with each other over drinks; it was good to see everyone. Later that night, I found myself, five years later, back at Tony's apartment with Migna, Tony, Tom, Joe, and others who stopped by to see us. Somehow, that day came full circle; I started my morning at the Millenium and ended my day above Jake's Saloon. Two years later, I had a job offer that took me to New Jersey. I had to wrestle with the idea of returning to the New York area, but did end up settling in New Jersey, first in Hoboken and then in Edgewater. Both locations are on the Hudson River, looking at Manhattan and the WTC site. I've loved living in the NYC area and have seen the resiliency of this city and their people.

The words "never forget" are so true. Every year around Labor Day, my stomach starts to drop, I get more anxious and feel agitated. The coverage of the September 11th Attacks starts showing up on CNN and I find myself watching it and crying. The first few years, I felt compelled to watch and treat the day with reverence. I also knew my emotions were heightened during this time. Watching and crying for me was cathartic and I wanted to show respect to all those people whose names were being read out that day.

For over ten years, I spent my 9/11 anniversaries mourning: I would get up in the morning and pray; maybe go to church; write in my journal about how grateful I was to be alive; then I would take the day off of work and watch the coverage from beginning to end. I wept with the families and the survivors. At the end of the coverage, I would have a glass of champagne and toast those who we lost and those who survived and be grateful for my life. One exception was in 2004, when I missed my usual routine due to being asked to be a bridesmaid by a friend from college. That was a tough one for me because I did want to support my friend, but I wasn't really there. Looking back, I'm not sure how I made it through the day and I'm grateful I had my sister as my date, for moral support. Eventually, I started spending the day as a day of service and volunteering, and for the last few years, I've gone to work. Wherever I am on 9/11, I always take the time at those fateful points in the morning to bow my head and acknowledge those who were lost and be grateful for life.

I have never really written this story before now, but one thing I always knew was how incredibly blessed I was through this whole experience. I was with Laura, who is a calm, level-headed person. The stairwell I walked down—after choosing to get my things and bypass the closer stairwell--was on the opposite side of the building from the impact, so there was no damage and minimal smoke. We found Don in the sea of humanity and his hotel was a few blocks away, which kept us safe. Even though my shoes broke, I was with a team that offered to carry me. An amazing group of New Yorkers and former Sidley employees took me in for the night, sat with me and cried with me; I will always be grateful to Migna, Tony, and Tom. I am grateful for those who were part of my journey after, from Laura, who got on a plane with me less than two weeks later so we could help the San Francisco office, to the team who traveled with me for two years. As my colleague, and fellow 9/11 survivor said, we worked hard and partied harder; it was an escape, and it was so needed at the time.

I think I finally had the answer to my question of "why did I survive that day" on November 3, 2016, when I got to meet my identical twin girls, Amelie & Bradyn. I am grateful for everything in my life and the amazing people who have been part of my journey. I will never forget.

AMERICAN PRIDE INC.

Millenium Hilton
Next to the World Trade Center

December 12, 2001

Re: Room # 2210

Dear Bridget Pakowski:

On behalf of our entire staff, we appreciate your patience as it relates to our efforts to cope with the aftermath of the September 11, 2001 tragedy. We have received inquiries regarding guest property left on the premises following the forced evacuation of the Hotel and we are still in the process of addressing the matter. Though the hotel remains within the restricted area, we are able to provide some information to you.

Please be aware that Hotel staff was not allowed to return to "Ground Zero" to protect the building until September 24th. Once permitted by government officials to enter the restricted area, we were able to establish a security and limited engineering presence at the front entrance to the Hotel. We have maintained access control functions from that date forward.

Unfortunately, when the World Trade Center Towers collapsed, a considerable volume of debris from those buildings and surrounding structures broke through hundreds of windows as well as the front entrance to the Hotel. Since September 24th, a series of structural and environmental tests have been conducted throughout the building. Tests have revealed that potentially dangerous environmental contaminants have entered the building from the collapsed and surrounding structures through the broken openings of our hotel. We have been advised that fabrics or porous items contaminated by this debris could pose a health risk. We have also been advised that it will not be possible to mail contaminated property back to owners. If you want to receive these goods notwithstanding their condition, it will be necessary to retrieve them personally or by an authorized representative.

Over the next few weeks, a bonded and qualified hazardous material firm will enter each guestroom, and where able to do so, conduct an inventory of guest property and determine which property is capable of being safely returned. As each room is serviced, we will provide you with the inventory of the property in your room.

Prior to our regaining possession of the property on September 24th, there was some loss of property due to circumstances beyond our control. When you receive the inventory, please contact Tom Roberts, Claims Manager at (303) 220-2394 with any questions regarding the inventory. If you have not already done so, we suggest that you immediately contact your insurance company.

Once again we apologize for any inconvenience caused as a result of these unfortunate circumstances, and our inability to safely recover your property at an earlier date. Obviously should you have any questions, please feel free to contact our office at (212) 872-7370. The inventory and notification process should be complete within the next 30 days.

Sincerely,

John Sweeney
General Manager

55 Church Street, New York, NY 10007-3100
Tel: +1 212 693 2001   Fax: +1 212 571 2316
Reservations: www.hilton.com or 1-800-HILTONS

2WTC 105TH FLOOR

by Joe Dittmar

My name is Joe Dittmar and I currently live about four miles from the beach in Lewes, Delaware. I'm a devoted husband to my best friend, Betty, have four super adult children, two fabulous sons-in-law, the best daughter-in-law ever, and four wonderful grandchildren: Alex (25), Jacob (10), and twins Nora and Joey the III, who are Covid-born miracles and only 15 months old. The blessing to have this wonderful family was nearly wrested away from me on September 11, 2001. At that time, I was a resident of Aurora, Illinois. I was working in downtown Chicago for CNA Insurance, so my being in New York on the 105th floor of the World Trade Center's (WTC) South Tower that day was a classic case of being in the wrong place at the wrong time. However, my surviving the catastrophic events of that day is also a life-altering event that had positive effects and changed my future significantly. I am so fortunate to be able to share my experiences of this, in this collection of stories, as well as doing presentations across the country about 9/11 and my experience--fifty to sixty times a year, pandemic notwithstanding. Let me share my story of that fateful day in the hopes that all of us will always remember and never forget!

As I mentioned, I'm in the insurance industry, and New York City, in particular, the WTC, has always been a mecca for this industry. Being in that business, it was not unusual for me to be in New York for a meeting. I started the morning of 9/11 in South Jersey. I got up at 3:30 in the morning to drive to Philadelphia, to take a Metroliner from Philly to New York City. As we were approaching the station in Newark, New Jersey, my cell phone rang and woke me. It was my wife back in Chicago. I said, "I'm glad you called; you woke me up. The train is pulling into Newark." She said, "I thought you were going to New York." I said, "Yes, but I'm going to the Trade Center, so it's just a lot easier to take the PATH over from Newark." So, I told my wife that morning, kind of by accident, that I was going to the WTC. I got off the train in Newark and took the PATH train over to 2 WTC, where we were going to meet at Aon Corporation's headquarters, which were on the 105th floor.

Mary was the facilitator of the meeting. She was a broker for Aon Corporation and somebody that we had all known for quite some time--a very powerful woman. So, it was quite strange when we got up to the conference room, and there's Mary with a bottle of liquid soap dusting furniture. Way out of character for Mary, this was not something that she would normally do, but, this was an important meeting for her. She wanted the place to look good.

At about 8:30 a.m., when the meeting was supposed to begin, nearly all the fifty-four attendees were there. We were in an enclosed conference room with no windows to the outside world. Like all insurance meetings, this one was starting a bit late. At about 8:48 a.m., the lights flickered. That's all. No sound of any sort, no sight of anything, just the flicker of the lights. Nobody thought a whole lot about it. Almost immediately, a gentleman by the name of Rick from Aon walked into the room. He looked at everybody and said, "Hey, I'm a volunteer fire marshal for the 105th, 104th, and 103rd floors here in the Trade Center at Aon, and there's been an explosion in the north tower. We've got to evacuate." Everybody in the room looked at Rick and kind of waved their hands. A couple people grumbled. The attitude was generally "Hey, we're here for a meeting, and we're fine. Nothing's going on; let us go." I remember thinking to myself, "Damn, I came all the way here from Chicago for this meeting, and now we're going to evacuate." It was just a feeling of aggravation, more than anything. Everybody grabbed for their left or right hip to retrieve their cell phones, so they could call and groan and moan to somebody about the fact that this meeting was potentially going to get canceled. Interestingly enough, the cells weren't working; we didn't know why not at that point.

When everybody was moaning and groaning, Rick said, "Hey, look, I can't leave until everybody leaves, and I want to leave." He said it with a smile, and that got everybody to get up and go. They herded us all down to the closest fire escape on the 105th floor to get out of the building. Yes, we were going to WALK down 105 flights of steps! Nobody knew what was going on. When we got down to the 90th floor, the door to the fire stairwell was propped open. Now, if you've ever been in a high-rise building, you know that if you look on the back of those doors, you'll see a sign that says something like, "Once you're in here, don't leave here. Go all the way down and exit at the lobby level." And here was this door propped open on the 90th floor, and everybody's heading out that door. I did what everybody else did; I followed them out. I should've known better, but I kept thinking to myself, "Hey, I don't know the building. Maybe I have to go to another fire escape some where and make a switch." I wasn't sure what was going on or why everybody was going out.

As soon as I got on the 90th floor, it became pretty evident what people were doing. It wound up being probably the thirty to forty worst seconds of my life, because that was the first opportunity we had to see the North Tower in an unbelievable state of tumult. The plumes of smoke were five, six, seven stories high, with flames redder than anything you've seen before, and the fire just spilling out of the building. It was a beautiful, clear day, and we clearly saw through the smoke and flames, and saw the signs of a fuselage of the plane. Being such a clear day, I remember immediately thinking, "God, how could this pilot have missed seeing this building?" The fact is, that pilot didn't miss; he knew exactly what he was determined to do. We saw the paper and the furniture and the people falling from the building, and it was an unbelievably gruesome sight. People on the 90th floor seemed to be almost mesmerized by the view. People were screaming, "Oh my God! Oh my God!" and every time we'd see somebody fall from the building, there'd be another shriek. And yet these people just seemed to be pressed to the glass to watch. I never got that close. I can't even watch a horror movie, and to see something like this...I knew this wasn't a made-for-TV movie, this was real life, and it scared me. And I thought to myself, "I'm not going to stay here."

Two extremely strong feelings took over my whole being at that time. One just made me go, "I want to get the hell out of here." But the other feeling that came over me almost immediately, as I'm seeing this gruesome sight through the window, was the feeling that I know everybody has; it's called the "I want my mommy" feeling. I just wanted to go home. So, I don't know--maybe I'm a big coward—but, at that point, I said, "I can't watch this anymore. I must leave. I have to get out of here." As I turned to go back to the fire escape, one of the guys that was in the meeting, Lud from the Zurich Insurance Co., said, "What are you going to do?" I said, "I'm going to get the hell out of here. What are you going to do?" And he said he was going to get out, too, but he explained to me that before he was going to go down ninety more flights of steps, he was going to go to the restroom. This guy made a simple decision--to go to the restroom--and he didn't get out that day. That simplest of decisions cost Lud his life.

I got back in the fire escape, and it was right at that point when the public announcement systems started to make the infamous announcement that said something to the effect of, "The event has been contained to the north tower. The south tower is safe. If you work in this building, we suggest that you go back to your workstation. If you're a visitor, we suggest that you stay where you are until further notice, but if you do feel you need to leave, please proceed with caution." I didn't hesitate. I was leaving, and I proceeded with caution. It was absolutely incredible to see the number of people in that stairwell who turned around at the 90th and proceeded to go back up to where they worked. I decided that I was going home. I wasn't going to stay. I had to leave.

I was approaching the 76th floor, one of two sky lobbies in the building. This presented us all with a chance to take extremely large, high-capacity express elevators to the ground level. Mary, our meeting host, was out in front of me and was hailing me to go the sky lobby and take the elevator with her and some others. Due to critical decision making, luck, or divine intervention—or all three--I made what became the best single decision I made this day, and maybe even in my life, up to that point. Being in the FIRE insurance business, it was <u>always</u> drummed into us that we would <u>always</u> recommend that people in a fire situation <u>always</u> avoid elevators and take the stairs. I thought of this immediately and made that decision, waving politely to Mary, without ever saying a word and continuing to go down the steps.

I was somewhere between the 74th and the 70th floors, when the second plane plowed into our building, though we didn't know what was happening at the time. I've never felt anything like that before, and I hope I never do again in my life. That stairwell literally shook from side to side, at what seemed like impossible angles. This building was rocking back and forth. The concrete was breaking; the handrails were breaking away from the concrete. The steps were waves undulating underneath our feet. Unbelievable. There was this heat ball that went blowing by us faster than I can say it, and you could smell the jet fuel. It seemed like it was going on for hours, but it was probably seconds or minutes. I was able to stay on my feet while this thing rocked back and forth. It's unbelievable how strong that building was to be able to take that; we didn't have a clue that our building had been struck.

About a flight-and-a-half of steps later, I caught up with Fred and Todd, the guys that I came into the meeting with that morning, and Fred was kind of picking himself up. Todd had already gotten up from falling, and they were dusting themselves off and getting themselves together. And you know what's weird? You would think when something like this had just happened, there would be all this screaming and panic and pandemonium. But, no--actually, the best way to describe it was just stunned silence. People had no clue. Once again, people were trying to use their cells, but their cells were gone. Actually, that probably was a good thing, because I think if we were able to call the people that we wanted to reach, the ones who we cared about the most--in my instance, my wife--it would have probably scared us more than helped us, because the people that were not in the building knew exactly what was going on. People were watching this live on television. We were in a concrete tower, and we had no clue. In our wildest dreams, we never thought that a plane had come into our building.

I found out later from the folks at *USA Today* that the heat, just from the friction of the plane through the building, was over 2,000 degrees Fahrenheit. So, all those people on the 78th floor, they didn't know what hit them. I guess that's a good thing, because there was no pain for them.

Even after the plane hit our building, the lights were on and some type of ventilation was working, because we were getting air in that tower and we weren't getting any smoke, other than that heat ball that flew by us and that little bit of jet fuel smell. We figured out later that we started on the 105th floor, the highest occupied floor in the building that day, so basically, there was nobody behind us. There just weren't that many people there. That was another reason why I don't think there was a lot of panic.

Fred had ripped his pants and suit when he fell down, and it was starting to get warm because we were huffing and puffing down a lot of steps. Fred had smoked in his earlier days, and it caught up with him. He had half a lung removed, so he was really struggling. He walked down two or three flights of steps, then he kind of wanted to quit. He'd say, "You guys go ahead." We wouldn't let him do that. We would coach and coax each other down. When we saw some people that were either a little bit overweight or partially handicapped, we were trying to encourage them too, "Come on. You can do it." They were wanting to quit, and we couldn't necessarily help by carrying them. What we could do was inspire them to continue. We couldn't run, so we kind of did this little skip thing going down the steps, trying to move as quickly as we could. We had never seen so many pairs of women's shoes in one place; it was absolutely incredible. But when you think about it, if you've got heels that are six inches tall and you're trying to go down seventy-eight flights of steps, you're certainly not going to wear those shoes. So, the shoes got removed and tossed to the side, and we were just kicking them out of the way. There were coats, briefcases, laptop bags with laptops, bags of food and all other types of items in that stairwell that folks discarded, in order to lighten the load. They didn't really impede our exiting, as the stairwell was wide enough for three to four people. We just pushed that stuff aside.

It wasn't until the 35th floor that we finally got a good sense of what was going on, because that was the first chance we had to run into the firefighters, police, and paramedics of NYC and The Port Authority. It's hard to talk about this because we realized, after the fact, that the looks on their faces meant they knew exactly what was going on. They knew that they were going up those stairs to fight a fire that they could not beat. They knew they were going up to try to save some lives they could not save. They knew that they were going into the bowels of hell, and they knew they were going up but not going to get out. They knew, and yet here they are, going up those steps. Unbelievable. I thank them for saving all those lives they did save that day. I mean, three thousand people lost their lives, but thousands and thousands of people were saved, including me. We owe those guys. We owe them not to ever forget.

We saw a guy that had been walking along with us, a maintenance guy from the building. The whole time, he had with him one of those phones that act like walkie-talkies. Right at the time we saw the firefighters and the police, this thing started to belch and beep and make all kinds of electronic noises, and we hear this voice screaming through the phone, "We're on eighty-two. We can't get down. We can't get down. We don't know what we're going to do!" And this guy stopped, turned around, and started to go back up the steps. He was right next to me, and I looked at him and said, "What are you going to do?" He said, "I don't know, man, but I got to go help my friend." If you want to know what an American hero is, that maintenance man is the true American hero. I mean, this guy was willing to lay down his life to save that of a friend. Just to be able to do that--the guts, the bravery, and the grit—for the love of another human being, it was hard to watch. I can only hope that guy got turned around by the cops and the firefighters later on.

Probably my favorite character was on the 15th floor, but we heard him from all the way on the 18th floor. It was a security guard, and he was singing. I mean he was singing at the top of his lungs, and he was singing "God Bless America," which was an unusual pick of a song, or so we thought. And he's singing this as loud as he can in this off-key way and he didn't even know all the words. In the middle of the singing, he'd stop, and he'd yell, "This is a day you'll never forget!" And then he'd sing a little bit more, real loud, and then he'd stop and say, "This is a day that's going to go down in history! And you'll be a part of it!" He just kept going on, and, you know, it was incredible. This was another guy that knew. He was sent up from probably the lobby level to get to the 15th floor, to make sure that people kept moving down that stairwell. It was kind of like the thing in the Titanic where they put the musicians up on the deck to keep people calm. This guy was singing and making cracks and making people laugh and making people think he's crazy, and what he was really doing is keeping people calm and saving lives. Incredible. Absolutely incredible.

When we got down to the lobby level, Fred went out of the door first, and he looked back at me and he said, "Hey, don't look left and don't look right." And when someone tells you to do that, you look left and right. I saw the carnage, the twisted steel, the concrete, and the red blotches--and we knew what the red blotches were. It was absolutely a horrific sight; it was like the ravages of war.

Because of all this mayhem and the sea of destruction outside our building, we could not leave the building at the ground level. Instead, we were directed to go down another set of steps and exit into the concourse, or the underground level of the WTC complex. This was the first time we encountered people who were adversely affected by the event; they were missing limbs, had gaping wounds--real blood and guts stuff. Your human nature pulls you to want to aid these folks. But on that day, we couldn't help, because there was so many fire fighters, cops and paramedics down there helping those who needed help the most. I've never seen in one place at the same time, such an outpouring of caring, concern and LOVE. That's what it was, a total outpouring of love.

So, the folks that needed help were getting the help they needed. Those of us who were okay? We were on our own; the herd mentality takes over and you hope that the lead person in your herd knows where they are going, because that concourse was a rat maze of corridors, fast food restaurants, coffee shops, boutiques and signs that meant absolutely nothing to you if you were not a New Yorker. A young guy in front of our group suggested we go to the most northeastern part of the complex, as it was an exit point that was the furthest away from the towers. This sounded right to my internal GPS, and I followed him.

When we got to the northeastern end of the complex, the escalators leading to the ground level were not escalating, so we climbed some more stairs and got to a street exit. All kinds of uniformed personnel were pushing stuff back away from the building with little Bobcat bulldozers. It was just gruesome to see what was on the ground. The cops were yelling at us, "Don't look back, just go. Run, run, run." You know, like Sodom and Gomorrah, somebody's telling you not to look back. You look back, and you see these buildings in an unbelievable state of duress. It was a tickertape of paper, furniture and bodies. It was incredible, absolutely incredible to see these buildings so torn apart.

On the escalator steps on the way up, I was fortunate enough to run into a business associate by the name of David. He stopped with me to look back at this scene and asked me where I was going to go. I told him the truth; I had no clue. My plan was to take a train from NYC back to Philadelphia, get in my rental car there, drive to Philly International and fly back home to Chicago. But I surmised, that's probably not going to happen. David agreed and suggested I start to walk with him to his condo on the Upper West Side.

We were about eight blocks north of the building, at a commercial laundry whose doors were open. We wanted to use their phone. They had their radio on, and they had the all-news stations on. That was the first opportunity we had to hear that this was an on-purpose terrorist attack, and our jaws just dropped to the ground. I remember thinking, "Not here, not in the States. This could never happen!" It was right at that time, that the two sounds that haunt me every day occurred. First, the sound of the twisting steel and crumbling concrete, and the building that we were just in--the south tower--falling to the ground. But, the sound that haunts me the most is the sound that I hear before I go to sleep at night and when I wake up in the morning: the sound of hundreds of thousands of people on the streets of New York all screaming a bloodcurdling scream at the same time.

Fearful of what may occur next, David quickly decided

that we could take cover in a friend's apartment nearby in the Tribeca section of the city, where we were. There, we did what everyone else in the country was doing; we watched TV, tried to understand what was actually occurring, and tried to figure out if it was safe to get out and go home. We tried calling our loved ones, but it was fruitless. Cell service was impossible because the main cell tower for southern Manhattan was on top of One WTC, which was now fully engulfed in flames at the highest level. Landlines were overmatched with all the communications traffic trying to get out of and into NYC.

About five or six hours into waiting for some direction, the mayor of New York appeared on TV and said that he understood that everyone just wanted to go home, and he was going to aid that by allowing the subways to re-open. This was an incredibly brave and strategic decision. David and I made the decision to try and get to the subway, to go to his home. We had also heard that Amtrak was bringing in empty trains and getting people out of the city. So, as we rode the subway, our train happened upon Penn Station, Amtrak. David knew I wanted to get out of New York and get as close to home as possible, even if that was just Philadelphia. We got off the subway together and, by pure luck, we happened upon a train that was getting ready to leave for Philly! When we came out from under the Hudson River, we looked back to see what had been that beautiful skyline, now just a pile of smoke. It was an eighty-minute trip from New York to Philly, and there was not a word in that crowded train. Not a word was spoken. It was just a stunned silence.

I took a rental car to my mom and dad's house, who still lived in Philly at that time. My mom was there to meet me on the steps of the house, giving me this big hug and kiss. I basically did what everybody else did that night; I went into that house and watched TV to try to understand what was going on. I passed out from pure exhaustion and trauma.

I got up the next morning and made the fourteen-hour

trip to Illinois in about eleven-and-a-half hours. I called everybody--anybody who cared to talk to me and who I thought I needed to talk to--every member of my family, even cousins, aunts, and uncles who I hadn't talked to in a long time. Word traveled fast. My mom and my wife had basically been able to tell everybody where I'd been and what had occurred. It was just good to talk to people, because there was a security in feeling that people cared. You find out who your friends are and who really loves you on days like that.

As I got closer to Aurora, I called my wife for about the thousandth time and I said, "Where are you?" She said, "I'm just getting ready to go to church because they're having a mass. I'll just wait for you if you're getting close." I said, "No. No, today's a good day to go to church. It's a good place to be. I'll meet you there." I drove up into the parking lot of the church, walked into the back of the church and opened the door to the main area. This place was just packed. These hundreds of people in the church were all staring back at me because they knew what had occurred. I looked over to the right, to the pew where we always sit, and there was my wife, with my kids and my family and my friends.

My wife is normally non-demonstrative, really quiet, but at that moment, she jumped over the back of the pew and ran to the back of the church and gave me this gigantic hug and kiss. And I knew at that moment that I was home.

I was home!

WTC (SUBWAY)

by Joe Chason

My name is Joseph Chason, and I grew up in the Mid-Hudson Valley, which is located about 1.5 hours north of New York City, on the Hudson River. The area has always been famous for its natural beauty, especially in the fall, when the foliage is in full bloom. It is also historically significant, as an area of early settlement known for numerous battles on and around the Hudson River. During the 80s and early 90s, a large technology company's presence in that area made it a flourishing suburb. Thanks to the job opportunities and services surrounding a strong local economy back then, many people didn't need to commute to New York City to earn good money. It was a terrific place to raise a family, enjoy the outdoors, and strike a good work/life balance. But, by the time I graduated high school, that company had severely downsized its presence there and abandoned most of the buildings it once used, hurting the area economically in a way it never fully recovered from.

Those of us who were lucky enough to go to college would typically be faced with a choice if we returned home: stay, move to a more established city where there would be more job opportunities, or move/commute to New York City. I decided that my best prospects were in New York City, so that's where I started my career. It wasn't an easy start. I couldn't afford to move there. The commute was long (and expensive), the hours were longer as I tried to advance as quickly as possible, and there wasn't much time left for socializing or recreation during the week.

Yet, there were certain things that drew me to New York City. It had a buzzing, bustling energy like nowhere else I had been, or have been since. There were also plenty of jobs, even for someone just out of college with little experience. It certainly wasn't ideal, but it felt like the right choice at the time. "If I can make it there, I can make it anywhere", right? Even with hindsight, it *was* the right choice. Working in New York City at that time was professionally rewarding, socially stimulating (with many great friends and memories made), mind-opening, skin-thickening, and culturally enriching. But emotionally... it was nothing short of devastating, because I'm a survivor of 9/11 and this is my story.

From 2000 through 2006, I was an employee of the law firm Sidley Austin, which was located in Midtown Manhattan, on the East Side, at the time. I worked in the IT department and my specializations were testing applications and deploying computer hardware and software. I also worked with our Chicago-headquartered IT team, to troubleshoot and test the corporate platform for the New York office. In 2001, Sidley Austin merged with a law firm named Brown and Wood, which was located in Building 1 of the World Trade Center (WTC), on floors 54 through 59. Due to my specialization, the Chicago corporate IT team tapped me as their local liaison during the merger, and I helped test Brown and Wood's legal applications on our platform.

Members of our New York team and the Chicago team were scheduled to participate in live training sessions in Building 2 of the WTC on September 11, 2001. During that time period, I was splitting my time between the Midtown office and 1 WTC. Only a few close friends and family members knew I was splitting my time between the two locations, because we spoke on a daily basis. They were the ones who would panic instantly on that fateful day.

The days leading up to September 11th were unseasonably

warm and sunny, with high temperatures in the 80. I distinctly remember a few of my colleagues and I eating lunch by the fountains in the plaza between Buildings 1 and 2 of the WTC, taking advantage of those last beautiful days before the abrupt change of weather likely to come. There was even a temporary stage set up in the plaza right next to 1 WTC, which hosted live music for all of us to enjoy. Looking back on it, the beautiful weather and the joyous music couldn't have been more contrasting, when juxtaposed with what took place on 9/11.

On the day of the attacks, I was commuting from my apartment in Tarrytown, NY, to the WTC for the training session scheduled at 9 a.m. For those of you who haven't experienced it, commuting to New York City can be a real grind. For me, it began with a 6 a.m. awakening to get ready for the day. What followed was a 15-minute walk down a steep hill to the Tarrytown train station, a 45-minute ride to Grand Central Terminal, and another 25-minute subway ride down to the WTC from there. The Dave Matthews song "Ants Marching" often went through my head as the throngs of commuters slowly marched up the platform to Grand Central Station. That day, I reached my final stop around 8:50 a.m. That left me just enough time to walk to 2 WTC in time for our training session, or so I thought.

Combine an exhausting commute, a sweltering subway station, and the fact that I was cutting it close to our training session's start time, and you might understand my initial reaction of irritation when I got off the train at Fulton Street. As I reached the stairs, people were backed up far more than normal. "What the hell?" I thought. "Let's go people!" But as I reached the last few steps of the subway exit, I realized what was holding people back. At the top of the Fulton Street subway exit was a direct view of 1 WTC, and it was on fire. I slowly walked toward the building, confused. I could see the fire and smoke billowing from the upper floors and thought that there must have been an accident or a fire that got out of control. I asked someone standing in the street what happened. He said a plane had crashed into

1 WTC, just minutes earlier. It didn't make sense. How could that have happened on such a clear day? I wondered if a small Cessna-sized plane had lost control.

If you never visited the World Trade Center, it may be hard for you to imagine why a small plane was the first to come to mind, but the two main buildings were *so* big and *so* tall. To put it in perspective, each floor was an acre in size, with 94 floors in WTC 1 and 110 floors in WTC 2. Only their sheer size could give the optical illusion of a small plane having hit where we would later learn a much larger plane (American Airlines Flight 11) had crashed. I immediately thought of the people on those upper floors and prayed that it had happened before most had arrived to work.

I started to worry about the safety of my colleagues in 1 WTC and those who might have been early to our training session in 2 WTC. I kept walking closer until I arrived in that very plaza where we had been dining and listening to live music days before. Staring up at 1 WTC from in front of the temporary stage, I started to see things that were hard for my mind to process. At first, it looked like objects coming out of the building: papers, perhaps some office furniture, and then--the worst thing I've ever witnessed--people falling from the building. When you see something like that, cognitive dissonance does its best to convince you that your eyes are mistaken. I, like many people around me, stared in shocked disbelief. Then, people around me started screaming, and more bodies started to fall--one even crashing through the tented roof of the music stage with a horrifying thud. My heart broke in that moment. Still thinking it was an accident, I tried to make sense of what was happening. I wondered if these people had been trapped above the impact of that small plane, and perhaps couldn't bear the thought of the flames reaching them; choosing instead to take their fate into their own hands and leave this earth on their terms. In that moment though, it was just so shocking and sad to witness. However, there was not much time to process it.

The police were trying to get people away from the building and out of harm's way, so I took a few steps back. Seconds later, my senses were overwhelmed by the loudest jet engine I've ever heard, followed by an explosion and a blast of heat on my face from the fireball above. At 9:03 a.m., the second plane (United Airlines Flight 175) crashed into the south side of WTC 2, at a much lower floor than the first had, and it came through the building in my general direction. I turned to run as fast as I could, knocking over the person who was right behind me. I rolled and cracked the bone on the outside of my ankle on the concrete, but I ignored it. I reached back to pick up the person I knocked over and we both ran away as fast as we could. In that moment, it became crystal clear that this was no accident, and that was definitely not a small plane--we were clearly being attacked.

Running back toward Fulton Street, I stopped about two blocks from the WTC, where I felt it was a safe enough distance from falling debris and somewhat out of the way of emergency services. I turned back toward the buildings and saw them both on fire. 1 WTC's fire was growing at an alarming pace and 2 WTC's fire was almost instantly beyond control. I started to walk north, devastated by the thought that any human beings would purposely cause this horrific situation. I pulled out my phone to try to call my family, but the cell phone Towers were overwhelmed, so there was no signal. I kept walking north toward the Midtown office, until I found a subway that would take me north faster. It ran for three stops before officials evacuated and shut down all subways. So, I kept walking and walking. I felt terrible knowing that my family was likely in a complete panic, having not heard from me for more than an hour after the attack.

As the Empire State Building came into view, I turned east to avoid it, in case that building was next to be attacked. That's when I felt the crunch in my ankle for the first time and it started to hurt; I suppose the adrenaline had finally worn off. I kept walking and trying my cell phone because the lines at the pay phones were extremely long. I finally got through to our Midtown office. I told them I was ok and that I was walking back as fast as I could; I could hear the relief in their voices. I asked that they contact my immediate family for me, which my colleague, Danielle, did.

I continued to walk back, heading further east to avoid Grand Central Terminal (another possible target, I thought). I watched fire trucks and police cars—so many of them--from Midtown and further north, speeding down toward the WTC, sirens blaring. Tears and sweat streaming down my face, I quietly begged them to turn back, knowing there was no hope of putting out such a fire; my wasted pleas drowned out by the wails of sirens. I feared they were all doomed; dutiful heroes rushing to certain death. I learned weeks later that entire departments had been lost, including one which I would walk past every day on my way to work for years after 9/11. I would often peek inside at the memorial and my heart would sink every time.

When I finally made it back to our Midtown office, the first thing I did was ask if everyone who was down there was ok and accounted for. I remember hugging some of my colleagues and shedding a few more tears with them. I learned that New York City wasn't the only target. I learned the Pentagon was also hit by American Airlines flight 77, causing 184 more patriots and civilians to be lost and striking at the very heart of our national defense. I learned about the heroes on United Airlines flight 93, who made the ultimate sacrifice to prevent terrorists from accomplishing their goal of further death and destruction, at the devastating cost of 40 more innocent lives.

It was all so surreal. I wondered how this could happen, what would be next, and when it would be over. At some point, someone wrapped my ankle with a bandage from a first aid kit and gave me an ice pack to stop the swelling. A few people who arrived later than I did were covered in ash and dust from the collapsing buildings. I vividly remember one of my closest colleagues, a tattooed military veteran named Rick, grabbing me by the shoulders, looking at me with tears in his eyes, and telling me that I too, had been to war. I didn't really understand what he meant at the time. Reflecting on it now, I think he was trying to prepare me for the post-traumatic stress that he had likely endured, and he wanted me to know that he was there if I needed to talk about my own.

At around 1 p.m., I decided that the whole situation was just too overwhelming and that I needed a drink to calm down. My friend Kristin and I headed down to Tammany Hall, the bar next door to our office where we'd spent many a happy hour, and we drank in sorrow instead. We drank a few martinis and we stared in disbelief as both Towers collapsed before our eyes on the TV screen; as the scarred Pentagon lay smoldering; as authorities searched the debris in a field in Pennsylvania. I would later learn that we lost one of our fellow employees in 1 WTC, a woman named Rosemary, may she rest in peace. I would also learn later that my friend Monica had lost her best friend, Shelly, may she rest in peace. September 11th happened one month after Shelly started a new job at Cantor Fitzgerald, the financial services firm that lost so many that day.

As the day wore on, I desperately wanted to get home to my family. However, the commuter trains were all shut down while the city tried to figure out whether or not there were more attacks coming and where the vulnerabilities were. Later in the evening, the trains started running again. As soon as I could, I took the train that would get me nearest to my mother's house, and spent the night there, surrounded by family. They greeted me with open arms and tears of sadness for what had transpired, mixed with tears of joy that I had survived.

Because my ankle was fractured, I did not return to work immediately, and went on temporary disability. Truth be told, I wasn't emotionally ready to return. I needed to get away from Manhattan for a bit and missed the rest of my immediate family, who lived in Florida at the time. I decided to drive to Florida and spend a few weeks with them while my ankle healed. In an act of selflessness, my mother gave me money for the journey, which was very helpful at the time. Although she couldn't really afford to do so, it was more important to her that I not return to New York City until I had time to process what happened, and until things settled down. She gently pushed me in the right direction, as mothers often do.

The nightmares began immediately and lasted for months. I couldn't watch any of the footage, which was constantly in the news. It caused flashbacks and more vivid nightmares. The rawness of the suffering of all those people was too much for me to handle, be it the poor souls who died from the impact of the planes, or the resulting fires; the people onboard those four planes who must have been so scared in their final moments; the first responders who lost their lives; and, of course, those poor people who jumped to their death. My nightmares were vivid because I *knew* those buildings. I had been in many of the offices and conference rooms on the 54th through 59th floors. I had been to Windows on the World for social events at the top of 1 WTC and taken in the majestic views from above. I had entered through the lobby of 1 WTC and ridden those elevators many times. I could picture in painful detail what these people had seen and suffered in their last moments, and that haunted me for a long time.

I returned to work about two weeks later, after my ankle had healed. I was able to find purpose (and distraction) in helping with the herculean effort of relocating all the Brown and Wood employees to our Midtown office building and getting the computer hardware and software they needed to continue their work.

In those early days after 9/11, I remember being so angry.

I was angry that so many lives had been cut short so senselessly and in such a violent manner, over stupid religious disagreements and ideologically-driven hatred. I recall instances of terror by mail using anthrax and talk of germ warfare being spread on the same commuter trains I used daily. I remember the shoe bomber incident and hoping if I were ever on a hijacked plane or train, I'd find the courage to step up like the heroes on United Airlines Flight 93 did in Pennsylvania. I remember experiencing anti-Muslim sentiment, which I'm ashamed of in hindsight. On my first train ride back to work, a Muslim man, dressed in full traditional garb, sat next to me on the train and started reading the Koran, while rocking back and forth in prayer. I remember leaning over and telling him that if he even reached for his shoes, I would break his neck. He didn't change seats; he just kept praying. I remember my mother getting kicked out of a restaurant for screaming at a man because she overheard him say that we deserved what happened on 9/11. Thankfully, those incidents passed, and the anger dwindled over time. Most of us knew it was not fair to overgeneralize and paint all people of Muslim faith as the enemy; yet so many of us succumbed to it in the heat of the moment. I also remember American Airlines Flight 587 crashing in Queens on November 12, 2001, shortly after takeoff, prompting the evacuation of the United Nations and the Empire State Building. We wondered for weeks if it had been another terrorist attack. It was a tremendously stressful time, but we endured the stress and went to work each day in defiance. I suppose it was our way of giving the collective middle finger to the terrorists.

 A few months later, I was asked by the Chicago-based corporate IT project team to travel all over the U.S. and abroad to help them upgrade the hardware and software for the entire global law firm. Strangely, with the intense focus on air travel safety, I had no reservations about flying. However, I was in a state of hypervigilance and always on the lookout for suspicious people when we did. I will forever be grateful to my friend,

Bridget, for selecting me to work on that project. Almost all the people in that team were at the World Trade Center on 9/11, and we had bonded in a way that would make that project both therapeutic and memorable. There is no doubt we worked hard (80 hours per week for 11 months straight), not only to deliver on the ambitious project, but maybe also to distract ourselves from what we had experienced. To balance out the long workdays, we would party just as hard in order to blow off steam and anesthetize ourselves. I think it's safe to say we had a bit of a carpe diem attitude going on, having seen how quickly life can be cut short.

On the first anniversary of 9/11, I was selfishly glad to be working on that large IT project in Los Angeles on Pacific Standard Time. I was grateful to be asleep during the remembrance ceremony because I still wasn't ready to watch all the footage. My friend, Nick (from our Chicago office) and I took the day off from the project, rented a convertible, drove up the California coast to Malibu for lunch, and visited my family in Camarillo. In a clear attempt at escapism, we did our best to distract ourselves, because we were not ready to relive that day.

Although I can't remember what I was doing on the second anniversary, I'm fairly certain I was still avoiding the television. At that point, I was also seeking therapy to deal with the nightmares. On the third anniversary, I was able to commemorate the day without triggering the nightmares I spent years trying to escape. I think I was finally able to visit the September 11 Memorial Reflecting Pools, also known at the 9/11 Memorial, on the fifth or sixth anniversary, and it was very moving. I went alone and walked to the fountains, located within the hallowed footprints of the gigantic buildings I used to stare up at in awe. The size of the pools and the fact that they are in the exact locations of the former buildings made them very visually impactful. The water falling down into the pools felt like the collective tears of everyone mourning those we lost. It took me 45 minutes to walk around each one and find the names I was seeking. Eventually, I found Rosemary's and Shelly's names and put my hand upon them both. I felt a connection. It felt like I was praying for each of them specifically in that moment. It felt like I was telling them each how sorry I was that this happened to them. My heart ached and I wept for them, for all those we tragically lost on that day, and for their loved ones.

Toward the end of that worldwide project there was a week of downtime between the UK and Hong Kong offices, so I took a personal vacation to Italy. I unwittingly arrived in Florence just before a large anti-capitalism protest, which was heavy on anti-American sentiment, for obvious reasons. A college-aged protester sitting next to me on the train said that we deserved 9/11 because of our capitalistic greed. I had to call the conductor and move my assigned seat before my emotions got the best of me. The conductor told me I'd be wise to leave Florence as soon as possible, or I might suffer similar encounters. I took his advice, running around the city as fast as I could the day before the protest and leaving the next morning. To be clear, having traveled to many places in the world, I am aware of the perspective of other countries on America, and I know that we have done some questionable things in our own self-interest. I also know that what we represent will always be loathsome to our enemies who don't share our beliefs. However, NOBODY deserved to die the way those people did --not in the name of ANYTHING or ANYONE--and I sure as hell let that girl on the train know it before I changed seats.

Even 20 years later, 9/11 continues to have a presence in my life, as I'm sure it does for many people. Personally, I still have anxiety about being on the higher floors of tall buildings and a fear of being trapped in a fire; I'm not sure either of those will ever go away. I learned at the 2009 Chicago Airshow that the sound of a loud jet triggers the memory of the second plane flying into tower 2. When a fighter jet passed by doing stunts over Lake Michigan, a panic attack washed over me and I walked home in a cold sweat, heart pounding. At least a few times every week, I will look at the clock and it will be 9:11 a.m./p.m., and I always heave a sigh at this recurring reminder. I have a very close friend and neighbor named Cheryl. She was engaged to a wonderful man named Paul who was tragically lost on that day, may he rest in peace. Although she doesn't speak of it too often, she knows I'm here for her if she ever needs someone with whom she can commiserate. I have another good friend who recently started spouting 9/11 conspiracy theories. I felt it was my duty to share my story with him and debunk some of those in real time, as a witness and as someone who knew most of those buildings quite well. He appreciated the honesty of the moment, agreed that he had some things to reconsider, and we're now closer friends for it.

When I visit my family in New York, I still occasionally visit The Rising, a 9/11 memorial in North White Plains, comprised of 109 intertwined strands of steel (like DNA), which rise 80 feet from the ground, reaching upward to the heavens. The intertwined steel rods exemplify the strength of the Westchester community and the families who lost loved ones. For me, it provides a local connection to people who lived in Westchester, like I did. I can relate to the journey those people took to work every day. Although I didn't personally know any of the people from Westchester who died, they could have just as easily been my neighbors. For me, the monument remains an easily accessible and moving way to remember 9/11.

These days, when I drive to our vacation home in eastern Washington, I drive past the Spirit of America 9/11 Memorial in Cashmere, Washington. I recently visited the memorial and found it to be a wonderful tribute to those we lost. The portion of a beam they have on display was from the 60th floor of one of the towers. They also have a beautiful set of bronze statues holding hands in a circle and staring up at the sky, which anybody can physically join due to one open space in the circle.

Photos of the 9/11 Spirit of America Memorial in Cashmere, Washington, taken by Joe Chason. *Memorial designed by Battle Ground sculptor Jim Demetro and his daughter Christina Demetro.*

https://911memorialwa.org/

I guess the point I'm trying to make is that I never have to look very far to reconnect with that day. It's somewhat omnipresent and I am at peace with that now. On a more positive note, I have a wonderful nephew named Joshua who lives in England and was born 9/11/2012. Celebrating his birthday every year brings light to an otherwise dark and difficult day.

The truth is, although it took me a few years to come to terms with what happened, I have lived a blessed life. Call it survivor's guilt, but it's really hard for me to say that in this context, knowing that so many people who also deserved to live blessed lives were denied that right on 9/11. I have travelled to many places in the world, including parts of Europe and Asia, which was a fun and eye-opening experience.

In the years that followed, I was able to contribute to a number of impactful projects during the rest of my tenure at Sidley, Austin, Brown and Wood. I subsequently enjoyed a rewarding global IT role at Deloitte, allowing me to travel to Prague every few weeks and work with some very special and talented people, many of whom remain close friends. I've since worked at a few IT companies and enjoyed a diverse, customer-centric career. I left New York in my early 30s and have lived in Chicago, Illinois and Dana Point, California, before settling down in the Seattle area. More importantly, I married my beautiful wife in 2012 and we have two wonderful children, ages eight and five. Thanks to the tremendous success of my wife, Jennifer, I'm currently on a temporary career hiatus so that I can be a stay-at-home dad--my favorite job yet. We still live in the Seattle area and love the scenic and active lifestyle here. I have many amazing friends and my extended family is largely healthy (thankfully), although my father did pass away in 2017 from cancer. I dearly miss him, and his phone calls every year on 9/11, when he would remind me how thankful he was that I was still here. I wish he were still here too.

Although bearing witness to 9-11 was a harrowing experience, I also learned a lot from that day and those that followed it. I learned how strong we are as a people, and how the United States (and the world) can really band together when times are tough. Sometimes I wish that it did not require tragedy to unify us all. I feel like we've forgotten what it's like to be united as a country since then, and we've truly suffered for it. I learned how important family and friends are, because mine were there for me to help me recover from the pain of that day.

On 9/11/2001, I learned that there are truly evil people in this world. On the very same day, I learned that real heroes *do* exist--people who run toward horrible situations and put their lives in danger to save others. I will always have a tremendous amount of respect for all first responders and those who serve our country. I learned that, although far from perfect, America stands for something special, which is unbreakable, no matter how hard others may try.

I struggled for quite some time to deal with what I saw that day. Sometimes I dealt with it in healthy ways (time with friends and family, meaningful productivity, therapy), and other times in less healthy ways (avoidance, drinking, overworking). It's also fair to say that the experience gave me an appreciation for the uncertainty of life, and how long it may or may not last. I'm sure many of us who were near the attacks have struggled with it in our own ways. Though there were some difficult times for me, I have always been keenly aware that others have suffered far more than I have, due to injury or the loss of a loved one on 9/11. To be honest, I'm not sure I would want any of them to read my story, because I don't want to reopen old wounds or detail what their loved ones may have endured in a way that causes them more pain.

Prior to writing this story, I never really thought about how precisely my time of arrival impacted what I witnessed that day. Given the fact that there were only about 180 seconds between my arrival and the second plane crashing into 2 WTC, there is no denying that I was meant to be a first-hand witness to a terribly sad moment in our history, and history (good or bad) needs to be preserved for future generations. It is for that reason I said "yes" to my good friend Don Bacso when he asked me to share this story. It was also important to me to make my contribution to the body of evidence that other eyewitnesses have created, so that what happened can never be denied, nor can related conspiracy theories be given any credence. We, the survivors, consider this part of our sacred duty to honor those who were lost.

I will certainly never forget 9/11/2001. We lost 2,977 innocent victims that day, and we've lost more first responders since then to disease from the toxic chemicals they were exposed to while performing the purely selfless and unimaginably heartbreaking task of clearing away the debris. I sometimes picture those we lost looking down upon us in the arms of angels, and I believe we owe it to them to hold their memory in our hearts, even if it hurts sometimes to do so. I know that I am only able to share my story with you because of where I happened to be, the moment it became clear we were under attack in New York City. This was a very difficult story to share, because even though it has been cathartic in some respects, it's hard not to relive the day as words are put to paper. Nevertheless, I hope that sharing my story helps to preserve the memory of what happened on this fateful day, and that we never see another one like it.

WTC (HOTEL)

by Damon Wilkinson

Written September 12, 2001

Wednesday night, 11:00 p.m.—So, people want to know what it was like at the World Trade Center yesterday. They want to know what happened, what I saw, what I think, etc. Well, I'll tell you what happened, but I'm going to tell you what it was really like, so if you don't want to hear the truth, don't read any further.

My alarm went off at 7:30 am Tuesday. I wanted to be in the office by 9 a.m. Between 8:30 and 8:40 I left to go to work. The office I was working in was on the 59th floor. I looked outside. It was a nice clear day, with none of the smog you see in Phoenix. I left my room and got in the elevator. I was on the 42nd floor of the Millenium Hilton, at 55 Church Street, directly across from the Plaza. I had an unobstructed view of the fountain and the plaza from my room.

We got in the elevator, and on the way down, the elevator did one of those big dips like it was temporarily off the track, then it corrected itself. I was in the elevator with a couple of other people. We all gave each other the nervous look everyone has when something like that happens. The doors opened at 37 even though no one had pressed that floor. I thought about getting off and taking a different elevator for half a second, but I decided I was being superstitious, so I rode the elevator down.

The doors opened at the bottom, and we came out into the lobby. I noticed that it didn't seem as bright and sunny as it had a few minutes ago. I wondered what had happened. Then I noticed a bunch of papers floating down. My first impression was that someone was throwing a ticker tape parade like you see in the movies. I thought, what a strange marketing blitz. I then saw a few people running around.

I went out the door to head over to work. At some point I thought that someone had broken a window and jumped out, but there were too many papers in the air for that.

When I got out on the street and looked up at the towers, I noticed smoke coming from one of them—the one I was supposed to be in.

My next thought was that a bomb had gone off in the upper reaches of the tower. I thought I should call my wife and let her know that I wasn't in the building. I figured the phone lines and cell services would start to be overwhelmed, and I should speak to her before she heard that something had happened at the WTC on the news or from someone else.

I called Tina and woke her up. I said something like, "The towers blew up, but I'm okay, I wasn't at work yet." She said "Huh?" so I repeated myself. I think I said, "Turn on the television, there should be something on momentarily." My next thought was to call some of my co-workers. There were two people I was working with who were staying in the same hotel as me. I tried to call Bridget's cell phone, but I couldn't get a signal, so I went back into the hotel to call Bridget's and Laura's rooms directly. I asked where a house phone was and they pointed, but the phones in the hotel lobby already had a long line. People were starting to pour out of the offices at the WTC. I realized that I had a landline in my room that would probably be working, so I got in the elevator and went back up to the 42nd floor.

I got up there, went to my room, and opened the blinds so I

could get a better view of the tower. I called Bridget's cell phone, got her voice mail, and left her a message to call me. I dialed the operator and asked for her room, but she wasn't there. I tried Laura's room and she wasn't there, either. I was looking up at the tower and the debris falling down. I'm guessing I was 100 to 200 yards from One World Trade Center. Two World Trade Center, the other tower, was basically the same distance away, only off to the left a little bit.

Stuff was falling from the top of the building. By now I could see a lot more smoke and I could see flames moving through the building.

I suddenly noticed three or four larger objects falling from the building.

They were people. I remember wondering, what is going to happen when they get farther down? So, I followed them all the way to the ground.

The first few people hit and blew apart like if you dropped fruit off of a rooftop. They left a large red stain on the ground. I noticed the torso of one person skitter in one direction while the legs went in another. This all happened in a second or two.

When my brain realized what my eyes were looking at, I yelled out. I quit watching the ground. I looked back up and more people were falling to their deaths. I didn't look at the plaza ground again. If I did, I didn't follow any more bodies to the point of impact; it seemed less horrible to see the bodies already on the ground than to watch them hit and blow apart.

Someone asked me later if they bounced. I don't want to talk about bouncing bodies, I only want to somehow register what I was looking at, and I want someone to tell me why I thought it was a good idea to watch these people all the way to the point of impact. Are we a morbid society? Am I a sick bastard? Why did I watch? Why did I continue to watch the whole thing?

Bodies continued to come down two and three at a time. A bullhorn on the street below came on to address the onlookers. "Please stay away from the building, debris is continuing to fall from the building."

Debris? These are people who chose to jump to their deaths, I assumed because that was better than staying where they were. How do you comprehend that type of decision? I had a later conversation with another person who asked why someone would jump. He thought they might have been blown out of the building instead and wanted to know if I could see where they had come from. I couldn't see anything. I just knew they were coming from the building. I'm glad I couldn't see anyone actually jump. They just appeared in my vision right below the fire line.

I thought they jumped because they were dying, either from the heat of the fire or smoke inhalation, and that they knew that by jumping from such a height they were likely to pass out before they hit the ground. Another friend of mine said later that maybe they could make peace on the way down. I really don't want to think about what these people were thinking about as they floated to their deaths.

Looking back, I'm more appalled that we had those conversations: here I am, chatting with people about why someone would jump or what they were thinking about on the way down. While I was looking out the window, I called my office in New York. When the receptionist answered the phone I said, "A bomb went off at the World Trade Center, and I'm watching bodies fall from the top." The phone went dead. I called back and said who I was. The receptionist said, "Oh my god, I thought you were a prank caller." I said no and told her to turn on a television right now. She transferred me and I spoke with one of my co-workers about something. I hardly remember what I said. I said I'd stay at the hotel for now. It seemed safer than going to the ground. It didn't occur to me that if the Tower collapsed it would easily hit my building if it fell the wrong way.

I changed the message on my cell phone to say, "I'm okay, I wasn't in the building. I'm in my hotel across the street. I can't get phone service; you can page me." Sometime after I changed the message (I have no idea what happened when from here on) the hotel intercom came on and said, "If you are still in the building, please leave." I thought, where am I going to go?

I had turned the TV on in the background and saw the tower on fire.

They had a helicopter viewpoint of the building on fire, and they were speaking with someone who was close. Some idiot reporter asked if they could see any people falling or if anyone was dead. I thought, Yeah, I can see people, and they are hitting the ground. Why don't I get a picture of that, you sick reporters? I'm sure I could take a great award-winning shot of the ground.

People were constantly falling by my window. As I said, I was on the 42nd floor, and I was looking up at the fire, so I saw them come down past me. I didn't follow any more of them all the way down, I just watched them float by my window. I remember wondering how long it took them to fall. I recalled what I mentioned above about people passing out when they jump from high enough. I was hoping these people were already unconscious. They floated by my window like leaves floating in the wind. I saw at least forty or fifty people go by.

I remember being outraged and thinking I should call one of the TV stations. I had a much better view than the reporters did, and I sure as hell wouldn't pull any punches about what I was seeing. I wondered if they would have the guts to let me tell it like I saw it, to not censor my comments.

A short while later the other building exploded.

I happened to be looking at Two World Trade Center. The

flames and smoke from One World Trade Center were getting a lot thicker, and I was wondering if the other building would get smoke damage or if the fire would cross over. From my viewpoint, I could see two sides of the South tower. I saw the two sides explode out in a massive fireball. I never saw the airplane. I thought it was a bomb going off, only this bomb was much lower, maybe around the fiftieth floor.

Smoke and fire rolled up the building, and papers and ash began to fall off to my left.

The intercom came on again and a voice said, "If you are still in the building, please come down and get out." I thought, okay, but I'm giving up my great vantage point. I wonder what it will be like on the ground.

Well, I better leave, I might get in trouble. Not get in trouble physically but get in trouble like in trouble with the hotel. What were they going to do, give me a pink slip?

It didn't occur to me to pack or grab my clothes or anything else. I just grabbed my briefcase; I wanted my laptop. I briefly wondered if I should take the elevator or the stairs. I started to grab the house phone to call the front desk and ask them, but then I decided that nothing had happened to my building, so I would take the elevator down.

When I got back down it was a lot darker outside. I was wondering what I should do next. I had left the upper floors like they asked me.

Should I hang out in the lobby, find another pay phone, or what?

They were evacuating people out to the side street, not Church Street but the other street there on the corner.

As I was walking out, some guy was talking to the hotel staff. He said he was supposed to check out that day and wanted to know if he should go up and pack. The hotel staff told him not to worry about checking out, just to leave. I realized I was supposed to check out the following day. I wondered if I would be able to get back into the building later, when everything calmed down. I thought they might block off the streets or something. I decided that since I had my hotel key, maybe they would let me back down with that. I asked someone from the hotel if there was a number I could call later. It's crazy, people are dying in the next block, and I am worried about my luggage. They said, "Here, take some stationary, it has the hotel number at the bottom, now get out." I grabbed the paper and went out the door.

I started walking up the side street. I didn't know where to go, but it made sense to get away, because they would most likely have rescue vehicles coming down soon, and I'd be in the way. Someone asked a cop where to go, and he said to get back behind some street. I couldn't hear him, but I assumed he meant the next block up, or the block behind the hotel.

As I was walking up the street, I saw a white piece of clothing in the road. It looked like a shawl or something, and there was a pool of blood under it and beside it. I remember thinking, that's too small to be a body. The police must have taken the corpse away already because the sight of that would make people upset.

People were in the street standing around, blocking traffic, getting in other peoples' way. A cop or someone near me yelled out, "What the hell are you looking at? People are dying up there and you want to watch the show? What is wrong with you? Get out of here!"

I kept walking up and took the first left. I don't know Manhattan, but I knew that left was uptown. I joined in the masses of people walking up the street. I went a block or two before I stopped to look at a map to confirm which way I was going. I thought about stopping some place where I could have a good view, but I realized that my cell phone battery was low, and people were going to be worried. And I would just be in the way when rescue vehicles arrived. I also remembered what the cop had yelled about watching the show and not realizing what I was really looking at. So, I decided to walk up to my office at 42nd and 5th Avenue. I was on Broadway, so it was a straight shot.

As I walked along all the people were talking about what they had seen, where they were, did anyone notice what had happened, etc. I passed some woman who was sitting on the street with a friend all panicked and hyperventilating. I remember thinking, What the hell is wrong with you? You weren't in the building, what are you worried about? I was across the street; I should have been in the first tower. Look at me, I'm fine.

What's your problem? What sort of sick thought is that? My pager started going off with new messages, and my phone started telling me, you have one new message, two messages, three messages—but it never rang, and I couldn't get a phone line out. I finally managed to get a line out and I told Tina that I was okay. I asked her to call both the New York office and the Houston office and tell them I was okay, and to tell New York I was walking there since my last message to them said I was in the hotel, and to tell Houston in general, because they'd figure out where I was and start to worry. Oh, and to call my friend who had paged me. She said sure and we hung up.

I managed to talk to a few other people while I was walking. When I got to Union Square, I could finally look back and see the buildings again. They were covered in smoke at the top. I turned around and the whole crowd gasped out loud. I turned back around and the top of the second tower was gone. I asked what happened and they said it just fell. I thought, Glad I left, I have to get to the office. Not anything else, not what happened to the people in the building, on the ground, my friends in the first building. Just, that's interesting, how do I get to 5th and 42nd? Bizarre.

I followed Broadway until it intersected with 5th Avenue. I followed 5th Avenue up. There was basically no traffic. All these pedestrians were just walking in the street, jaywalking. It's not like there was any traffic to hit us. At some point on the walk the first tower collapsed.

Again, everyone around me yelled, so I turned around and saw the cloud of dust go up. I turned back around and kept walking toward the New York office. I eventually got to the office and sent out an email that I was okay.

The rest of my day is not worth writing about, other than some random thoughts: Buildings are gone, tons of people are dead, yet I kept wondering about my hotel, if I could go back down there to get my luggage. My luggage. Who cares? Rationally, it doesn't matter; it's just clothes, shoes, ties, a couple of books. Yet emotionally, I want my stuff back.

How messed up is that thought?

I also thought that, as bad as it sounds, part of me was glad that the plaza was covered in rubble. There would be many dead bodies, but you have no idea what it looked like to see the bodies of the people who jumped. I thought while I was walking up the street that I was sorry someone was going to have to see those horrible sights to clean up, but that at least those people were trained to see that. I'm glad a building collapsed with thousands of people in it so we wouldn't have to see a gory plaza. It's not rational, it's stupid. But that's what I thought.

The rest of the day I watched TV: idiot reporters talking about death tolls and confirmed dead. I wanted to call in and shout at them, ask them if they knew how repulsive, idiotic, and stupid they were. I've often thought reporters at certain events asked stupid questions. I wished someone would punch them out or tell them off or something, and if they were dumb enough to ask me or talk to me, I would tell them way more than they ever wanted to hear.

As I've tried to get home for the last day and a half, I've thought about what that first plane flight after all this would be like. My friends got out of the WTC. They decided they were going to rent a car and drive home to Chicago. I still have no idea when I can go home. My friends offered me a ride, but driving to Chicago doesn't get me any closer, so I thanked them and decided I'd take my chances in NYC.

The really sick thing now is part of me is wondering what it was like to go down the stairs. Was it cool, was it neat, was it a wild panic, what was it like? I'm a nosy person and can ask questions, fish for details and find things out, but other than a general response, I don't want to know what it was like. I saw some horrible things and I can only assume they had a worse experience. I don't want to know the details. I sure as hell can't relate, so why bother having that empathetic piss-poor cocktail party conversation: "Oh really? Oh, that must have been horrible, you poor thing." What the hell kind of stupid comment is that? So, I don't want the details.

I did have one conversation with one of my three friends. I asked her how long it took them to get out, how did they leave, and where did they go. I want to talk about what I saw, but the people who weren't there don't get it. They most likely will never get it, and now I know what some people mean when they try to talk to me about things I've never seen but then I try to relate to it. You just can't. I mentioned to my friend that from my hotel room I could see the entire plaza, I had an unobstructed view, and I had seen some not so pleasant things.

She said yeah, on the concourse level they had seen some not so pleasant things also. That's it. I don't want to know any more.

What's sick and twisted is part of me does want to know more—just like you guys think I had some really interesting experience, and you want to hear all about it. What is wrong with me, and what is wrong with us that you want to hear the details? Don't ask me about it. If you've read this far, then I think you've figured out it was a horrible day. You know that I'm a big talker, I love to talk, but not this time.

Some things are better left unspoken.

THE RESPONSE IN THE MIDWEST

by Nick Maviano

In September, 2001, I was 28 years old and just shy of my second anniversary at Sidley Austin, LLP as the IT trainer and Project Manager. I was responsible for new project training of staff and had started working towards IT project management within the firm, specifically a new Windows image that was to be piloted in our offices at the World Trade Center (WTC). My manager, Bridget, and four of my colleagues were already in New York for this implementation. I was scheduled to fly there the following week; this week, I stayed in Chicago to train fall associates.

The morning of September 11, 2001, was a perfect, sunny, fall day in Chicago. During the typical workweek, while getting ready in the morning, I always listened to a CD and then my Mini-Disc player on the twenty-five-minute train ride to work. Due to my daily routine, I did not hear or listen to any news before arriving to the office. I would later learn that during my commute, the first plane hit the WTC; no one on the train knew, as these were the days before smart phones. I arrived at my office building on West Monroe in the Loop at around 8:25 a.m. and went to my office on the 20th floor.

Things appeared a bit odd when I was walking in; my co-workers were all gathered around a computer, looking concerned and scared.

"Did you hear what happened, Nick?" my co-worker asked.

I responded, "What are you talking about?"

"An airplane just hit the World Trade Center, where our New York office is!"

After that, I went numb, knowing that my co-workers and friends were in the WTC. I ran to my computer and pulled up MSNBC.com and saw the photo of the WTC building exploding. I couldn't believe my eyes. It wasn't real; my mind could not immediately wrap itself around this. I was in shock and full of adrenaline, but I remember thinking that it must be an accident. It just did not seem realistic to me.

We were asked to come up to the 22nd floor, where most of the IT department was located. We gathered around a computer and had one of our co-workers from our Dallas office on speakerphone. Within minutes, my colleague and friend in Texas yelled, "They just hit the second tower!"

It just was not real; my 28-year-old brain was not equipped yet to fully grasp the severity of what was happening. I remember realizing this was a terrorist attack, but the office was moving at such a rapid pace that I just did not have time to process. I knew my friends were in the building and the main focus was trying to locate and make sure our colleagues were accounted for and safe--not an easy task during these unprecedented minutes.

We immediately went into crisis mode, trying to find out where all our colleagues from Chicago were. We tried the office phone numbers, everyone's cell phones, email, and AOL instant messaging, but all were busy or not responding. At around 9:40 a.m., the news confirmed it was a terrorist attack, and reported that the Pentagon was hit, and the plane in Pennsylvania was reported down. Again, my brain was just trying to comprehend what was happening to the U.S.A. at this point.

We were all asked to go into our offices and keep trying to call our co-workers in the WTC. I remember trying to find my manager's family's contact information, to see if they had heard from her, but could not find any details online or in her office, so I just kept calling her cell phone and getting busy signals. About twenty minutes later, Bridget called my office, crying hysterically. I was so relieved to hear her voice, but my stomach dropped as I started imagining what she and my other friends had just gone through.

"We can't get a hold of anyone, and the cell phones are not working," Bridget said, calling me from a payphone. She was with Laura and Don, two of our Chicago colleagues. "We need you to conference in each of our families to let them know we are okay."

So, one by one, that is what I did. I started with Bridget's calling her mom and dad. The tears were gut-wrenching, but the sound of her parents learning she was okay was comforting. Then, we moved on to Laura's family and finally Don's. Each call was about five minutes in length, and I remember hoping that the call would not get dropped. During the conversations, everyone was crying, including me. Hearing, "I love you so much!" from all parties involved really showed that in life, and especially at that moment, that was all that mattered.

After talking with each family member, the New York team was heading up north to a co-worker's apartment for safety and we said our goodbyes for the morning. My heart was racing as I looked online at MSNBC and thinking over and over what was said on each call to their families; "I love you!" was said over and over by everyone. The images were beyond belief to me--explosions, people running, the towers on fire. It was truly a real-life disaster movie, without the special effects. Again, I just felt stunned, I was looking at the images, but could not believe this was happening. Directly after this call, I let our IT Director know that I was able to speak with the team. I stayed on the 22nd floor for another twenty-five minutes, watching the news, before we were asked to evacuate the Loop for safety reasons, thinking Chicago could be a potential target.

I took a ten-minute taxi ride home to my apartment, as I did not feel safe on the train. As soon as I got to my apartment, I called my parents and broke down. They were relieved I was out of the city and back in Lincoln Park, and we talked several more times that day. The bustling neighborhood that I lived in was eerily quiet that day; I assumed most people were inside their homes watching the news, as I was.

My roommate got home, and we could not turn off the TV the entire day. Reality was starting to set in on what had transpired that morning. The news repeatedly showed the explosions, the towers falling, and people running, calling it the worst terrorist attack America had ever faced. As the day turned into night, the pit in my stomach continued to get worse; my anxiety was out of control. I popped an Ambien around 10 p.m., as I knew I would not sleep--I just wanted to get back in the office the next day and help the best that I could from Chicago.

The next morning, I woke up early to watch the news and took the train back to the office. We all gathered in a large conference room to plan how to get the New York office back up and running from another location. My co-workers in New York were heading back home in a car they had rented, and restoration work began. By Monday, my boss returned to the office, and I remember giving her a huge hug. I could tell she did not want to talk too much about what she had gone through, and I respected that.

The following week, many Chicago colleagues headed out to New York by car to help get a new office up and running. I was asked to go to London to get a satellite office, which was connected to the WTC, started. I remember flying out in late September, after travel restrictions lifted, and having a knot in my stomach the entire flight, but I knew this was nothing in comparison to what my co-workers went through in New York.

Looking back, at age forty-eight versus twenty-eight, I have a better grasp of life-and-death situations and what is truly important--and what is not--in this world. At the end of the day, surround yourself with good people that care about you and the rest should take care of itself. Do not let the little things or negativity in life upset you, as they are all little things. Focus on what makes you and your loved ones fulfilled and happy.

Lastly, I should now add that ever since 9/11, the first thing I do when I wake up in the morning is grab my iPhone and look at the news.

THE PENTAGON

Built as a rush project in World War II to house the rapidly expanding War Department, the Pentagon is immense, with five floors above ground, five concentric rings, 10 radiating corridors leading from a central 5-acre pentagon-shaped interior courtyard. The Building, as it is commonly referred to by those who have worked there, has 17.5 _miles_ of corridors, some 20,000 doors, and more than 6.5 million square feet of office space. While just over a quarter mile across, its design makes it quick and easy for someone to get from the farthest point to the opposite side of the Building within 3-5 minutes at normal walking speed. Each exterior face is 907 feet long, and 62 feet high. The corridors were wide and there were stairs and ramps throughout the Building, and elevators and escalators were exceedingly rare. The Pentagon had workspace for more than 23,000 people to be on duty, and the Building had cafeterias, cafés, coffee shops, and other amenities to support such a robust workforce.

AMERICAN PRIDE INC.

PLAN OF THE BUILDING - FIRST FLOOR

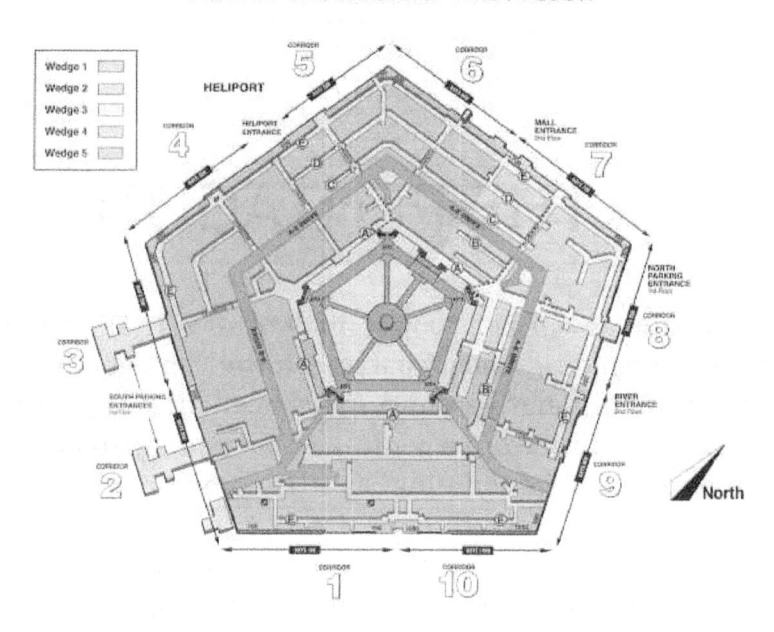

Diagram courtesy of the Historical Office, Office of the Secretary of Defense, Pentagon 9/11, 2007, page 7

PENTAGON

by Ryan Yantis

My name is Ryan Yantis. On September 11, 2001, I was a 40-year-old Army major, 14 months into a 36-month Pentagon assignment on the Army Staff. I had 8 years of experience as a Public Affairs Officer (PAO) following 8 years as a Cavalryman before my Pentagon assignment. In the Pentagon, I was an Army spokesman. I led a team of other media relations specialist, in explaining the Army's wide-reaching personnel policies and practices developed by the Army Staff and the Secretary of the Army. Originally from Northern California, I entered the Army in Columbia Missouri, served in Europe, South Korea, and the continental United States (CONUS), as well as deployments to Africa (1994) and Bosnia (1995-96). I was married and lived in Dale City, Virginia, and had two young children, a four-year-old and ten-month-old.

I want to start my story by telling you about the Pentagon. It is an amazing and exceptionally large building. The geography of the place played a large role in my daily duties and was one of the reasons I was not killed or injured on 9/11. It was just luck and being stubborn, in equal measures.

I worked in a shared office space for the Media Relations Division in room 2E636. This alphanumeric was not only the room number but provided directions to how to get to the office. This meant it our office was on the 2nd floor, E Ring (outermost ring), near Corridor 6. Since the specific office room number was

36, it told someone seeking it to get on the 2nd floor, on Corridor 6, and walk to the E-Ring. Once there, since the last two numbers were less than 50, turn left and start looking for the door number. 1D451, would be First Floor, D-Ring, on Corridor Four, and then right to room 51. In 2001 the doors were vintage from generations before, with wood and security glass, and some with transoms. Generally, these doors were well-worn and had thick layers of either varnish or paint, quaint in appearance in a modern building setting.

My team and I shared office space with other Public Affairs Specialists, assigned to the Media Relations Division (MRD) of the Office of the Chief of Public Affairs (OCPA). There were 16 of us assigned and on duty on 9/11, and we worked in three main team assignments.

The Operations, Intelligence and Logistics Team (OIL Team) was focused on the "warfighting" sections of the Army staff and Secretariat. The Weapons, Environment & Technology Team (WET Team; also jokingly referred to as the Science Club) supported those sections of the Army Pentagon that dealt with weapons system development, production, acquisition, existing and emerging technologies, the Army Corps of Engineers, and the Army's environmental policies and practices. My team, the PERS Team, supported the Army staff in all matters pertaining to "people" and human resources in the Army.

While the PERS Team assignment may have sounded boring and innocuous, we handled *people* issues – the good, the bad, the ugly, and far too often the *very* ugly. We responded to media queries and prepared press releases on topic such as promotions, weight control policy, explaining how the Army was implementing President Clinton's *"Don't Ask, Don't Tell"* policy on homosexuals in the service, as well as Army casualties (deaths and serious injuries), high-profile acts by or against Army personnel, and legal matters about our people, Army-wide. We also handled high-profile misconduct situations, investigations, prosecutions and good order and discipline personnel issues (sexual misconduct, rapes, murders, murder\suicides, etc.) So, for the PERS Team, with 1.3 million men and women in the Army at that time, <u>every day</u> was an opportunity for a one-in-a-million event to happen, and pretty much did. Some of these were profoundly serious, heartbreaking, and some amazing in their complexity and exploration of human nature and the foibles of people.

The PERS Team area was at the rear of the MRD space in four low-wall cubicles where we could see each other from our desks. Each desk was a gunmetal gray typical government type that had been around since the 1940s or 50s, with huge multi-line phones and an almost obsolete desktop computer with a big screen at each station. Many desks also sported a small TV with a 9-inch screen where up to four different news stations could be playing at the same time on screen, with one audio feed. Mine was typically either on CNN or Fox News out of New York City; on 9/11, it was *Fox and Friends*.

The WET and OIL Teams had a similar layout and space, and our MRD division chief had a private office. There was a meeting/waiting area where we could talk to news media near the entrance to the MRD office space, with a large flat panel TV mounted on the wall between MRD and the adjacent Community Relations division. The part of the Pentagon that housed our offices was old and tired, with layers of paint, construction, and improvements. It had a feel of a well-used and worn-down office with hand-me-down furnishings and equipment. Having worked in New York City for two years immediately before my Pentagon sentence, I was expecting better.

PENTAGON EXTERIOR

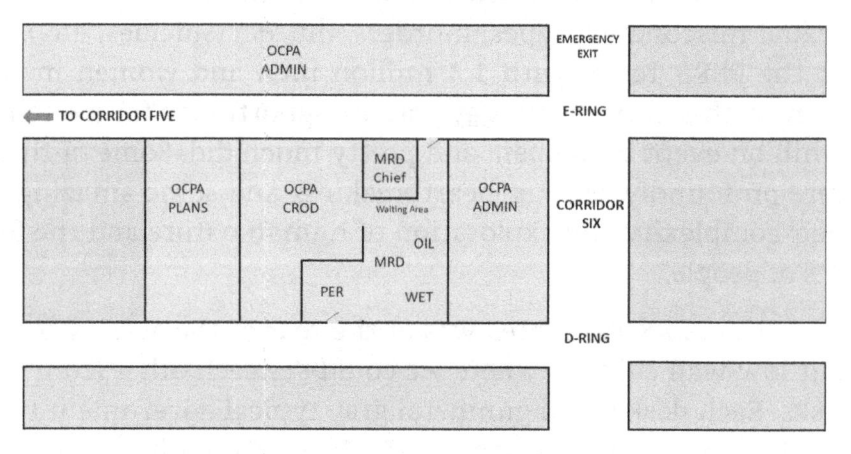

```
┌─────────────────────────────┬──────────┬──────────┐
│           OCPA              │EMERGENCY │          │
│           ADMIN             │  EXIT    │          │
│                             │          │          │
├─────────────────────────────┤  E-RING  ├──────────┤
│⟵ TO CORRIDOR FIVE           │          │          │
├──────┬──────┬───────┬───────┤          │          │
│      │      │ MRD   │       │          │          │
│      │      │ Chief │       │          │          │
│ OCPA │ OCPA │       │ OCPA  │ CORRIDOR │          │
│ PLANS│ CROD │Waiting│ ADMIN │   SIX    │          │
│      │      │ Area  │       │          │          │
│      │      ├───┬───┤       │          │          │
│      │      │   │OIL│       │          │          │
│      │      │MRD│   │       │          │          │
│      │      ├───┼───┤       │          │          │
│      │      │PER│WET│       │          │          │
├──────┴──────┴───┴───┴───────┤  D-RING  ├──────────┤
│                             │          │          │
│                             │          │          │
└─────────────────────────────┴──────────┴──────────┘
```

Image prepared by the author, Ryan Yantis, March 2021

This is my account of the 9/11 Pentagon Attack. I never wanted to be assigned to the Pentagon, but there I was, working in "the Building".

Tuesday, September 11, 2001, started as a beautiful day. The clear blue skies held low humidity, and the temperatures were forecasted to be a perfect day to go play golf. But instead of playing golf it was a weekday morning, so I went to work in the Pentagon. My normal arrival time to the Pentagon was about 7:00 a.m. I remember getting in, checking email and reading overseas and overnight news, and preparing myself for another routine day. The team leaders had a standard morning meeting with our Colonel to discuss anticipated media events and actions in his office. Our MRD boss was an Army Colonel, and we discussed what media events, talking points and challenges we had in detail, and about the media queries and actions each of the three teams - OIL, WET and my PERS Team were facing or anticipating. Theis meeting started at 7:30 a.m. that day, but ran well over our normal 30 minutes, easily more than an hour.

I remember returning to my desk after the meeting where on my small TV I saw the initial news reports of a plane having hit a World Trade Center building in New York City. Initially, I thought it had to be an accident, as the flight path into LaGuardia was over Manhattan, and bad things can happen to good people. As usual, the first news reports were sketchy and not clear on the type of plane involved at that time, with *"...situation unfolding, we will report as the details emerge..."*.

I remember checking for news reports on my computer while listening to the TV at the same time trying to understand what was happening. I also tried to make sure that everybody in my office knew that something bad was happening in New York City. I called a few Army people I knew New York City to make sure that they were aware and were safe.

By 9:00 a.m. most of the available MRD team member were watching the big TV near the front of the office, learning about the events in New York City. There were six or seven of us, watching live reports about the World Trade Center. There was a certain amount of disbelief and chatter as we watched what was unfolding on TV. At 9:03 a.m., I recall seeing the second aircraft flying in from the left side of the screen to the right and striking 2 World Trade Center (South Tower).

There was a collective gasp, some cursing, and expressions of disbelief in reaction. A young, blonde college intern who was on her second day of a 16-week internship was seated, watching the TV. She had a shocked and scared expression and had started to tear up. I had met her the day before and in a "tough love" attitude I told her toughen up and get back to work as we were going to be busy that day. I also reminded her that she had said she wanted to see and do exciting things, and to just wait.

One of my PERS teammates was Elaine Kanellis. Elaine was a very experienced and savvy Department of the Army Civilian employee, and she was in her ninth month of pregnancy. Elaine was a key part of my team and our overall office, bringing immense communications expertise and skills to bear on a wide range of topics. She knew the Army Staff well and was a trusted and respected player in public relations and representing the Army. She had good connections with people in the Building who were interested in getting things done, and done right.

"Elaine, please get your stuff and go home," I said. "I don't want to have to worry about you."

"But Ryan, we are going to get slammed today (by all the media queries). You are going to need me. I want to stay and help."

"Elaine, get your stuff and go, please," I replied. "We're next."

This was a hunch I suddenly had that the attackers, whoever they were, were going after signature targets; symbols of American power and might. The Pentagon was a visible symbol of American and western power and might.

We discussed her leaving for a bit, but events began unfolding quickly. There were media calls coming in, and activity quickly ramped up. In between rushed conversations and terse instructions, our nation was under attack, and we had work to do.

Lt. Col. Henry Huntley, our OIL Team leader and deputy division chief, was newly assigned to the Pentagon and had been with us for just over 6 weeks. I remember him asking me if my last assignment had been in New York City, which it had. Would I be available to attend a meeting with him at 9:30 a.m., to discuss what help to provide, if New York asked for military assistance? The DOMS meeting – *Domestic Operations Military Support* – was a routine response to situations such as major events, natural disasters, hurricanes, large-scale fires, etc., where local and regional resources would be overwhelmed. While the military cannot send in troops without invitation or authorization, we could and did contingency plan for emerging situations. The attacks in New York were such a case.

Shortly before 9:30 a.m., Henry Huntley and I walked quickly down the wide, quiet hallway of the E-Ring, heading toward Wedge One, the recently renovated section of the Pentagon. Surprisingly, there was a normal, routine feel to our walk. The Pentagon was humming along, with people carrying out their normal, daily actions.

When the Pentagon's construction started on September 11, 1941, Wedge One was the first segment built, largely from poured and formed concrete, with wide hallways, ramps, and the best technology of the 1930's. When renovations started in late 1998, Wedge One was the first to be renovated with many new features, including a different floor plan. Our MRD office was in Wedge Two, and we were slated to move into new spaces in Wedge One, but there had been delays.

As we walked on the Pentagon's wide terrazzo hallway, Henry and I discussed possible support New York City might need. He asked me about the World Trade Center buildings and complex; had I ever been there? Yes. How busy are they? Very and with the time of the plane strikes with pedestrians on the streets below, the falling glass and debris could have injured many, many people.

About then we found ourselves at a construction door which marked the boundary from Wedge One to Wedge Two on the E-Ring, or the outer ring of the Pentagon. This heavy gunmetal gray double door gave me an opportunity to ask where we were going.

"A conference room off of Corridor Four," Henry replied

"Great. What's the address, Sir?" I asked.

"I'm not sure; we will find it," Henry said.

I quicky reminded him there were five floors and five rings on Corridor Four, and that the new layout was different than what we were used to. We determined we did not know the room

AMERICAN PRIDE INC.

number or who was hosting the meeting, and after a spirited conversation we agreed to call for information. We ducked into a nearby office and called. It was then just 9:30 a.m. - when the meeting was scheduled to start. *Great,* I thought. *We are going to be late.* I hate being late. Then with the information we needed, we walked quickly to the Army Operation Center (AOC) which was at the base of Corridor Seven.

As we entered the AOC, a secure vault-like facility in the Pentagon, alarms blared, and I recall a light flashing. Over the din, an Army sergeant looked up from his post at the security desk, and hanging up the phone said "Gentlemen, there has been an explosion. You need to evacuate the Building."

There was a pause as the news set in. Henry and I both asked at the same time for more information, and where the explosion was.

"Near the helipad," the sergeant simply said and went back to his phone, answering calls.

The helipad was outside the Pentagon, between Corridors Four and Five, just where Henry and I were standing, minutes before.

In the AOC at Corridor Seven there had been no physical sensation of the attack. Other than the alarm sounding, I did not hear an explosion or any kind of impact. But now that we knew where the incident was, Henry and I quickly conferred. He was going to stay in the AOC and get more information, and as the AOC was part of his teams' media responsibilities, it made sense. I wanted to get back up and check on our people, and my team, to make sure they were safe and got out to the Pentagon. As I left the AOC, Mike Conroy, a civilian assigned to Henry's OIL team walked in. I told Mike I was going back to check our office and what I knew about the attack and told him to head out and to use the Corridor Eight exit, as it was closest to where we were.

As I left the AOC, I worked my way along the D-Ring to the

stairs on Corridor Six, and then to the second floor. There were men and women, military and civilian pouring out from their offices and heading towards the exits. While there was rapid movement, I do not recall seeing or hearing panic, or anyone yelling. I pressed my way forward through the bustle of people in the now-crowded hall. Once I was on the second floor on Corridor Six, a well-dressed woman in business attire was walking quickly towards the A-Ring, her high heel shoes click-clacking on the wide polished terrazzo floor, and I could hear her sobbing. I then rounded the corner at the E-Ring, and in a few moments since the alarm had sounded, I re-entered the MRD office space.

It was eerie. The lights were on, the computers were on, and phones were ringing, but there were no people at their desks. It seemed as if every phone in the office was ringing at the same time. Alone, I walked through the office to my team's area wanting to check on my teammates and to get my stuff. Elaine was not there. Was she safe? Did she go home, as I had asked?

My desk phone was ringing. Since I wanted to make a quick call, I answered it. A reporter was calling with a routine question about an Army personnel policy. I replied that I did not have time to take his query right then, as the Pentagon had apparently been attacked. He asked if I would talk about that. I said "no, not really" and hung up. As I hung up, the phone rang again and I answered. It was another reporter with another routine question that I declined to answer. When I hung up the second time, I got a dial tone and an outside line.

I quickly called my home. When my wife answered, I let her know that I was alive and was going to get out of the Pentagon. She had questions, but I did not have answers, just that I was okay and that I was heading out of the building. She asked me to check in later, so I unplugged my personal cell phone and slid it into my pants pocket.

Then I noticed that there was what looked to be sand and small flecks of concrete dust on my desk. I was confused. My desk was almost always messy, but not dirty. Where did this *schmutz* come from? I looked up above my desk, seeing for the first time a spiderweb of cracks in the ceiling above my desk, running throughout our offices. The Pentagon was largely built of poured, formed reinforced concrete, both walls and floors. The floors on one level were the ceilings on the level below. I also saw hazy smoke and then could smell the hot and oily odor that was coming down from the ceiling. As I left our office space, I saw that the haze was thicker.

In the adjacent offices I checked for others. We had an employee of Department of the Army who worked in there and had special needs. As a young adult, she had some sort of accident and had challenges to her cognitive abilities. Sometimes, when she got scared or confused, she would revert back to some other level of experience. Instead of evacuating during a fire drill, she would "duck and cover". Fortunately, she was not there. I quickly checked the next office space. No one was there either. I went across the hallway to the Chief of Public Affairs office which was also empty.

Going back and forth across the E Ring and heading towards Corridor 5, checking offices to make sure no one was trapped or not aware of the situation, I did not find anyone. However, every time I went into the E-Ring hallway a security guard at the Corridor 6 emergency exit behind me would call out, "Hey! You need to exit the building!", which I ignored and continued checking offices. About the time I got to the corner between Corridors Five and Six on the E-Ring, I heard a deep, hollow THUMP. Seconds later, a large roll of dark, thick smoke came around the corner. It was much darker and thicker than the haze had been in the E Ring. I remember it almost being black and looking deadly.

As it rolled towards me along the ceiling, I stopped, and I took inventory. Here I was, wearing the Army Class B uniform, the duty uniform of the day, consisting of a short sleeve pale green uniform shirt, with a plain white T-shirt underneath, tucked into the dark green polyester and wool slacks. On my feet were rubber-soled Corfams, black dress shoes with high-gloss shine. These were a common footwear for military personnel in the Pentagon. The shoes looked nice and tended to be quieter for walking in the Pentagon's wide, quiet hallways. They are not great for running though, and certainly not great for going into a fire. It was then that I realized I was ill-dressed and ill-equipped to deal with a fire and heavy smoke. Then I heard the guard yell at me one more time from behind, and I did what he asked.

I left the Building.

In that moment, I felt I was turning my back on people in need. I really did not like that feeling. Even though it was the right thing to do, it is something that still haunts me.

***

Walking out of the Corridor Six doors, I recall the brightness of a sunny warm day. The air was warm, and as I walked quickly away from the building, with the sunlight on my head and shoulders. Heading west toward Virginia State Route 27, I walked quickly to our rally point for the Army Public Affairs office personnel about 150 yards west of the Pentagon. As I passed the corner of the Pentagon and could see down the western face of the building, I could see where the plane had struck the Pentagon.

It seemed to me that the entire western face of the Pentagon – the side with Corridor Four and Five - was on fire. There were at least two trees burning, and heavy smoke billowed into the clear blue sky. A large fire truck sat near the helipad, engulfed in angry orange and red flames, giving off black sooty smoke. In the neatly clipped grass of the grounds to the south of me, there were sparkles of light, and hundreds, if not thousands of pieces of debris – remains of what I later learned was American Airlines Flight 77, the airplane that had struck the Pentagon at 9:37 am.

Some pieces were large, while most were small.

Amid the scattered and twisted aircraft wreckage on the grass, men and women in uniform and in civilian clothes were walking and running from and to the Pentagon. Some were helping or carrying the injured to safety. A fire truck rumbled across the grass and stopped in front of the fire, spraying white foam from a roof-mounted monitor. I know there had to be the sounds of sirens, vehicles, people and the fire, but all I remember was silence, as if I was not processing the sounds correctly.

Debris covering the Heliport area Image from the Pentagon on 9/11, photo credits DoD image 2001

At our rally point was Sergeant Major Phil Prater. He was the senior noncommissioned officer for the Army Public Affairs, and personnel accountability – making sure all our people had made it out of the building was part of his responsibility. He was listing the people that he saw on a clipboard, and we quickly conferred. As he added my name to his list, I told him there was no one left in our offices, but that I had seen Henry Huntley and Mike Conroy after the Attack in the AOC. Since I had told Mike to leave the Pentagon by Corridor 8, Phil and I exchanged cell phone numbers. I then took off towards the Corridor 8 Entrance to see if I could find any of our other people for accountability.

Moving quickly around the Pentagon's exterior to the Corridor 8 Entrance, it was incongruent how beautiful the day was, while the death and destruction was on the western side of the Building. The Pentagon's grounds were well-maintained and, in many ways, park-like, with professional landscaping and good upkeep. When I got near Corridor 8, I stopped under the shade of a large tree to catch my breath. There, in a neat row at my feet lay 6 stretchers, in a row, open and ready for use. The stretchers were the classic military type – olive drab (OD) green canvas with OD green wooden side rails and handles.

I recall looking up the sidewalk towards the Pentagon and seeing three men in uniform clumsily carrying something between them as they walked towards me.

Realizing they were likely carrying someone in an improvised stretcher – a blanket carry; to use a Boy Scout term – I grabbed one of the available military stretchers in front of me and ran to them. The three men were carrying a severely injured young lady out of the building, and we quickly set her on the Army stretcher. The four of us then carried her to a nearby first aid point that had been established that morning, after the attack.

For the next 45 minutes time seemed to dilate to me, and it felt as if I was on autopilot. I was doing things and making things happen without thinking long or hard about what or why, just trying to help people. It was a blur of running, carrying people to safety and the first aid point, helping to move people away from the Pentagon. I was about 50 feet from the Corridor 8 entrance to the Pentagon; sweaty, footsore, and tired. I was heading back into the Building on an elevated walkway with the intent of helping others when the Pentagon security personnel started yelling to *get back!* Another plane was coming in.

It was then that I heard the jet, low and fast from behind, from the north. A powerful roar of engines screaming and echoing back from the slab face of the Pentagon limestone façade assaulted my ears. In the second it took me to stop and look up, the adrenaline rush of fear was immense and powerful. There was nowhere to run – fast enough or far enough – to get away from the Pentagon if another plane was going to strike the building.

Instead of a hijacked commercial jetliner, the sleek underbelly of a U.S. Air Force jet fighter flashed fast and low overhead, clawing upward through the billowing smoke from the fires on the west side of the Pentagon.

Relief flooded over me. We were safe, for now. We had air cover, and someone was looking out for us. The sun was shining, and I was still breathing. Now to get back into the Building and to rescue those trapped and needing help. I headed in. I was not alone.

***

The reason there was a first aid point established on the grounds near the Corridor Eight or River Entrance also had to do with the internal geography of the Pentagon. The Army's DiLorenzo Tricare Health Clinic was located 2E8 – the North Parking entrance to the Pentagon - and provided routine and urgent care for most military personnel assigned to the Pentagon. The clinic's staff included doctors, nurses, medics, and administrative and support personnel. Ironically, in May 2001, the Pentagon's Air Force Flight Medicine Clinic and the DiLorenzo Clinic teamed up with and the nearby Arlington County Emergency Medical Services and conducted a tabletop training exercise for a mass casualty scenario at the Pentagon. The premise of the exercise was that a commercial aircraft, on takeoff from nearby Reagan National Airport would have a bird strike and accidentally hit the Building. The casualties estimated from the exercise were 187 killed, ironic due to the outcome of the 9/11 Attack, but it also helped the medical personnel prepare.

In this situation, the plane hit on the E-Ring near Corridor Four on a shallow angle towards Corridor Five. The plane would push through three rings, creating a large circular hole in the C-Ring in the space between B-Ring. Those injured and able from the E-Ring tended to evacuate outwards, while those on the interior headed into the inner courtyard. The medics and other volunteer first responders surged into the courtyard and brought them to the Corridor 8 exit.

In the initial moments after Flight 77's impact, there was a real concern that another plane was inbound, either for the Pentagon, or another target in the National Capital Region (NCR), i.e., Washington DC. After a very short time of helping to get people out to the Pentagon, we had to shift our efforts and help move patients and the medical first aid point farther away from the Pentagon. We did this while cars were trying to leave North parking, and with traffic on the surface streets near the Pentagon. It was very hot, confusing work.

The medical folks needed more supplies from the DiLorenzo Clinic, so 30 to 40 people – men, women, military and civilian -- went back into the Clinic and took everything and anything that looked remotely useful or helpful. I recall seeing Henry Huntley there, also helping to get things from the clinic. I was very happy to see he was alive and well. We took anything and everything that looked remotely like it would help. There was a spirited effort to wrench a medicine cabinet that was locked from the very secure wall mountings, but that was unsuccessful.

I carried an armload of three portable oxygen tanks out of the clinic to the aid station, only to learn two were empty. A young Army specialist came out, carrying a prepped medical procedure tray, draped and sealed in plastic, with a light green cloth covering. As he handed it to the nurse nearby, he said he hoped it would be of help, and she graciously thanked him. I heard her comment to another nurse as he turned away that a Pap Smear test kit was not going to be of much use. Well, at least we tried.

We had the challenge of getting ambulances back to the north side of the Pentagon, as all the EMS seemed to be responding to the west side where the plane hit. My cell phone was not able to connect to a cell tower, and the medical and other Pentagon staff were trying to get ambulances to our injured. Meanwhile some cars would pull up and load up all the injured they could safely take and head off to the nearby hospitals. A new model minivan pulled up, and the driver hopped out, pulled all the seats from the back, and took a load to safety.

Suddenly, ambulances arrived in numbers and quickly loaded and departed with our injured colleagues. I was walking back into the Pentagon when the jet fighter roared overhead, which was trigger for us to get back into trying to help get people out.

Shortly after the medical staff and the volunteers, including me, picked up everything we had and thought we could use and headed back into the Pentagon, through the Corridor Eight entrance. Inside the building was dark, as the power was off. Only the sunlight filtering in from the doors and the battery-powered emergency lights mounted on the walls lit the way for us to walk through the building and into the 5-acre inner courtyard. The air was thick with heavy, acrid smoke, which made breathing and speaking difficult. We passed through Corridor Eight quickly and quietly.

The Pentagon's inner courtyard is a large open-air "no salute" area. A beautifully maintained park-like space of grass, trees and concrete walkways, it was a place where Pentagon personnel could get some fresh air, relax, or even enjoy a snack or lunch from the Ground Zero Café. It was a pentagon-shaped fast-food stand in the center of the 5-acre inner courtyard. It was nicknamed the Ground Zero Café as a legacy of the Cold War, and the practice of aiming for center of mass of targets. The joke was that the Soviets likely had a missile or bomb targeted on the Pentagon, and that the Ground Zero Café, would be just that – the aiming point – Ground Zero.

We quietly and quickly walked past the Ground Zero Café and unloaded all the medical materials and equipment we had carried into the courtyard. Here again there were amusing moments, as a large OD green fiberglass box one person had carried in was found to have training aids for medical situations. Nice, but not useful right then. I noticed there was a fire truck parked near the Corridor Four entrance, and that the firefighters seemed to be having trouble getting in and staying in the building due to the heat and smoke.

*Volunteers and emergency responders offer aid in the Inner Courtyard
Image from Pentagon 9/11, DoD image 2001.*

We unloaded the stretcher that we had carried in, and then moved off, closer to the Ground Zero Café, and became an Aid and Litter Team. The sun, now nearing its noon zenith was hot, and the air was very smoky. Visibility was a matter of a few feet. A medic was paired up with us, and the gentleman on the other end of the stretcher and I took a short break. He was wearing a suit and had credentials hanging from a lanyard around his neck. He pulled out a battered pack of cigarettes, and I asked him for one. Giving me one, we shook hands, and introduced ourselves. He was a reporter from the Washington Post, and was driving by the Pentagon when it was hit. He was there to help he said, not to cover or report. Fine with me, and thanks for the smoke I replied.

Soon after a young Navy officer came up and asked me for my t-shirt. Not knowing why it was needed, I took off my uniform shirt, and stripped away my sweaty, wet (and likely smelly) t-shirt. I handed it over, asking if we were short on bandages. The officer did not answer, but instead walked over and dunked my t-shirt in a bucket of water by the Ground Zero Café's back door. Now it was my turn to ask questions, so tucking in my shirt, sans t-shirt, I asked the sailor if she was okay, and what was she doing with my shirt.

She took my wet t-shirt and pulled it over her head, pulling it down so her face peered out of the sleeve. She then gathered up her should-length brunette hair in the wet fabric and contained her hair – in my now-wet t-shirt. I asked again if she was okay and she said yes, she was fine, the t-shirt would help with flash burns, and that she was on a search and rescue team.

Flummoxed, I was impressed with my Navy counterpart. She was maybe 5 foot 5, and slim, wearing a long-sleeve back wool and nylon sweater, with a knee-length skirt. She was wearing my wet t-shirt to protect her hair and head from burns if and when she went back into the building. Unlike the Army, the

Navy trains personnel extensively for firefighting, as fire kills ships, and it is always a long way to swim if you have to abandon ship.

Her actions and willingness that day made a huge impression on me.

The next several hours were frustrating and maddening. The fire and smoke were too hot for the professional fire fighters, all geared up to spend more than a few minutes in the Pentagon's smoke and death-filled halls. We waited, smoked, and asked each other, and any newcomers to the courtyard for news. Rumors were rampant. There was talk that there had been a truck bomb at the State Department, that all the aircraft were not passenger aircraft, but cargo. There was talk about other targets having been hit, and a lot of BS. Facts, other than what we could see with our own eyes were scarce.

There were several officers in the courtyard I knew from the office of Lt. General Maude, the Deputy Chief of Staff for Personnel (DCSPER). The DCSPER offices had recently moved into Wedge One on the west side of the Pentagon, near Corridor Four on the second floor. When I asked about people from the DCSPER team, most of the responses were grim or silent. One young female Captain was the DCSPER PAO, and a friend. She had worked closely with my PER team on a wide range of media questions and issues. I asked about her, but no one had seen her or heard from her. By end of the day on 9/11, her status was DUSTWUN (Duty Status and Whereabouts Unknown).

During this pause, I noticed there were quite a few Army Chaplains in the courtyard, including some I had previously worked with and advised on media issues. Some I knew were not assigned to the Pentagon, and I started talking with them. By chance, there had been an administrative board for the Chaplains Corps being held in Crystal City Virginia, about a mile south of the Pentagon. When they heard about the attack on the Pentagon, they ran to be present and to share in the danger and hardship. Chaplains serve in a ministry of presence, to be with those in harm's way, or under adverse conditions, to support, and, to share hardships. In this they lead, by supporting and serving.

Until mid-afternoon that day, time lagged and drew out. We were hot, tired and thirsty, and several vending machines were forced open for drinks. We waited, we watched, and we worried. The fire remained too hot, the smoke too dense, and we were not offering much to the effort. A female Army colonel had been sitting in the sun, her head down and motionless for quite a while. I went over to ask her if everything was okay. She looked up, a beatific smile crossing her face.

"Everything is fine, thank you. I was just praying," she was a Chaplain. At least she knew what she was doing.

A few FBI agents came into the courtyard, escorted by military personnel and Pentagon security. They talked with several of us and asked us to look for aircraft parts or other items that might be evidence in the courtyard. We were given some small flags on wire to push into the ground near any items we thought would be of interest. We did was asked of us.

***

Later in the afternoon we were gathered and told that we were needed on the west side of the Pentagon, at what was being termed the Impact Site. It was the first time I recall being told what to do or where to go by anyone in authority that day. Dutifully, we loaded up our stuff and walked out one of the southern exits, then around the Pentagon until we were on the west side.

Near the Impact Site, there were more people lined up as we had been in the courtyard. There were also more fire, EMS, and law enforcement. There were larger firetrucks spraying water on the Pentagon, including an area where the building had collapsed, which was an unpleasant surprise to many of us.

My boss and I saw each other, and he said he was heading back into the AOC. He told me to come as well, as it was now time to get back to being a PAO.

The AOC was a hive of busy activity, with officers and civilians talking and working on gaining information and preparing for a 6:00 p.m. briefing to the Secretary of the Army and the Chief of Staff. All operations centers take some time to coalesce and to harmonize, and the AOC was not in harmony that day. Tempers were short, people were tired, a bit flustered and short with each other. I found myself seated at a computer, having been directed to prepare a list of those we knew were dead or missing. I objected, as personnel status is a statutory action, and these determinations are made carefully, so as to not strip personnel of status and legal protections. Also, we never wanted to notify a family of someone dying on duty via a press release or through the media. There was a tried and proven method for notifying and supporting the next of kin of our fallen. But there I was, a major, being coached and supervised by way too many colonels and others, telling me how to do my job. The advice being put the names on the list by rank; no, list them by officer, enlisted or civilian; or alphabetically, my choice and instinct. I was chafing under all this conflicting guidance. I did not like it at all.

Suddenly the officers behind me fell silent, and a booming voice said to the effect, "Leave him alone to do his job. Oh, and list the names alphabetically. We are one Army. They all matter." I later was told that voice belonged to the Vice Chief of Staff of the Army, General Jack Keane. I was very grateful for this input and guidance.

The personnel team from DCSPER also weighed in and supported my assertion that it was too soon and improper to prepare any kind of list of those dead or injured. We needed to follow protocol and procedure, to ensure that identifications were made, notifications were complete, and that our fallen brothers and sisters and their families were taken care of. There was also no certainty of how many people had been killed or injured in the attack. Estimates were guesses at this point, and we started working on how we would have people check in to regain accountability.

We were working on establishing a phone bank for people to call and "report in" their status, when a young brigadier general started hollering about standardizing the font, size and background for the PowerPoint briefing slides for the evening update to the Army leadership. That was enough BS for me. I took a break to get something to eat and drink.

Coming back, I was tasked to be the lead escort to bring the Pentagon Press Corps and other media into the Pentagon for a press conference planned for just after 6:00 p.m. that evening. Since I knew many, if not all of the Pentagon Press Corps, I went with other available PAOs to the River Entrance, the ceremonial doors midway between Corridors Eight and Nine, where the Secretary of Defense would greet visiting dignitaries. There was tight and nervous armed security, including a magnetometer, and the news media quickly went through that tight security to enter a building that was still burning.

The press conference was held in the Pentagon Press Briefing room, to a capacity audience. Secretary Rumsfeld was joined by Secretary of the Army Tom White, Gen. Hugh Shelton, Chairman of the Joint Chiefs of Staff; the Chairman of the Senate Armed Services Committee, Michigan Democrat Carl Levin; and Virginia Sen. John Warner, the committee's ranking Republican.

*SecArmy White, Gen Shelton, SecDef Rumsfeld, Sen. Warner & Sen. Levin
Public domain photograph from defenseimagery.mil, 2001*

Mr. Rumsfeld said, "The Pentagon is functioning. It will be in business tomorrow." There were many questions on the damage, the number of killed, injured and missing, and not too many details provided. The Pentagon Press Corps, many who had been in the Pentagon when it was hit, and able to also know more about what was happening in New York and Shanksville, were not being combative or investigatory. Simply having the press conference there and then was very heartening and very much proof of life.

After escorting the news media out of the Pentagon, I returned and spoke with my boss. He told me I was emergency essential and to get home and get some food and rest. Our duty uniform for the near future would be the camouflage field uniform – the Battle Dress Utilities (BDUs). In this decision I was elated, as the BDUs are vastly more practical and comfortable than the Class B uniform.

There was only one problem with me leaving the Pentagon that night. All my stuff – my wallet, my keys, my cell phone charger – were still in my office, just off of Corridor Six. The FBI and others had blocked off the Impact Area and other spaces as it was now a crime scene. I needed to get in and get my stuff, as did the others still there from Public Affairs.

In the darkened hallways, young soldiers stood guard, standing in front of the yellow and black crime scene tape. I found a clipboard, a hard hat, and borrowed a flashlight from one of the DoD press liaisons. Talking quickly with others from the Army PAO office, I got a list of what they needed, and where it was at in our offices. One gent tried to tell me to check the fax machine for media queries, and to see if his computer was still running, and to empty the small fridge near his office so it would not get funky before we could clean it out properly. A more senior officer reminded him sharply that there were an unknown number of dead bodies in the Pentagon, and that one funky fridge was not going to be an issue. "Ryan," she said. "Go get your stuff and get my stuff as well." She let me start on my attempt to get through the MPs and into our offices.

Armed with the list, the clipboard, flashlight, and hard hat, I approached the young MP and told him I needed to look at something near Corridor Six. I guess I looked official enough, and he let me pass, asking that I be careful since things might have shifted or become unstable there. The visit to our offices was unremarkable, save that it was dark, smoky and without power, differently eerie than earlier that day. I gathered all the items and returned to my teammates. The funky refrigerator remained untouched by me that evening.

After getting people their stuff, I hustled to what I later learned was the last METRO train on the Blue line heading south. METRO is the subway/light rail system in the District of Columbia. On my was to the train, I called home and let my wife know I was heading for the Franconia-Springfield station, some 14 miles from our house. It was as close as I could get given the situation. The car was empty except for one or two other riders. We rode in silence towards home.

Getting into the minivan with my spouse and kids, I realized for the first time just how badly I smelled. We kept the windows cracked as we drove home and I stripped down in the garage, dumping off my smelly nasty clothes there. Into a shower, I scrubbed and got cleaned up, then food, then sleep, after making sure my BDUs were ready for the morning. It was going to be an early wake up on September 12.

Returning to the Pentagon

Far too early the next morning I headed back to the Pentagon, to report for duty. Expecting a long drive and rush-hour traffic, I was up, dressed and out of my house in Dale City, Virginia by 4:45 a.m., hoping to be at the Pentagon before 7:00 a.m.

Much to my surprise, I was virtually alone in my 25-mile drive into the District on I-395. As I crested the rise just south of my destination, to the north, in the pre-dawn darkness through my windshield, I saw the Pentagon. My eyes were first drawn to the side where American Airlines Flight 77 had hit less than 24 hours before, killing a then unknown number of people.

The Pentagon was still burning. I saw a glow coming from the impact area and water being sprayed on it. A gentle west wind pushed smoke across the top of the building and towards Washington DC. The southern section of the Pentagon facing me was black and without power. On the southeastern corner was the Corridor 2 entrance, one of the normal entrances to the building. It was brightly lit — brighter than normal — with large temporary flood lights that were deployed.

Coming off the freeway, I found the Pentagon's South Parking lot to be closed, with stern and grim-faced security officers directing us to park father away from the building. I parked as close as I could and walked towards the Corridor 2 entrance. For the first time in my assignment there, I was wearing the Army's camouflage field uniform, as our normal Class B "business" uniforms were not going to be appropriate for our new working conditions. It was still dark as I made my way through the pedestrian viaduct under the freeway, into the Pentagon's huge and eerily empty South Parking lot.

I walked north across the wide and empty expanse of a parking lot, normally packed full of cars. Out of the darkness to my left and right, others appeared as we neared the steps up to the Corridor 2 entrance. Men and women were walking briskly in silence, but with purpose. There was no chatter or laughter, just an occasional subdued greeting. There were well over one hundred men and women of all races, uniforms of all services, and civilians in jeans and blazers.

Up the stairs we went, finding the elevated Corridor 2 entrance to now be an enhanced security station, with security dogs to sniff people and bags, a magnetometer portal to check for weapons, and quite a number of well-armed, tense and focused security personnel watching everyone closely. We passively lined up, submitting to security checks to enter a building still on fire and largely without power to do our jobs. Looking back over South Parking, even more were coming behind us, also coming to serve. It was nearing 0600. Time to get to work.

Kudos to First Responders and law enforcement officers. They run towards danger. They wear protective gear, body armor, and carry the tools of their trades. They save lives and make a difference.

But how many calmly walk through smoke to go to work, largely shuffling paper and helping leaders make good decisions? That morning was an excellent example of service, duty, and servant leadership.

I was very proud of all those people then, and still am today.

September 12, 2001 was my Day One back in the Building and on duty I was on duty for the following 38 days, and I know I was not alone. Others came back to work on differing schedules as workspace and capabilities grew. As the Army Public Affairs work offices were off-limits for the time being, we borrowed desks, computers, and space to resume our mission and to communicate with the American people about their Army.

Good news emerged, as I learned Elaine had made it safely

from the building, and that she and her unborn baby were fine. She would work from an Army office in the DC area until her maternity leave.

Trisha Shaffer, the young blonde intern who was new to the Pentagon returned to duty a few days later and was an amazing young member of our team. She had an extraordinarily strong work ethic, an infectious, positive attitude and was willing to take on new challenges. She quickly transformed into a full member of our team, helping with media questions and other duties. She also took over the mail distribution for a bit, until we learned that there was anthrax being mailed to media and government officials.

Tricia Shaffer and Ryan Yantis, Pentagon Pressroom, December 2001, US Army photo 2001

Others in our team came back to work in the Pentagon, some after working remotely or in other Army offices nearby. For all that Day One, each person's first day back in Pentagon was tough. It was compounded by the time and emotional distance the early returners already had. We had overcome the raw emotions and the turmoil related to coming back into the Pentagon.

The Army and other services formed and employed Crisis Action Teams of mental health professionals, Army Chaplains and others to help individuals and teams to process the grief, uncertainty, and new reality of working in a badly damaged Pentagon. It was very helpful and reminded all that healing and a return to normalcy would take time, patience and understanding. Meanwhile, there was much work to do.

We were assigned a workspace suitable for four people, with about 20 people coming in on a daily basis. We triaged the media calls. Henry Huntley and I took turns taking queries and assigning action officers to handle the media. Phones and computers were at a premium, and we learned our email and electronic file were – for now – not available, as the server room with our information was damaged by water used to fight the fires. We reverted to much simpler methods and retail person-to-person media facilitation.

The Pentagon Press Corp and the other news media were keen to interview the injured survivors as well as the families of those who had died and had been identified. We did the best we could to help our comrades and their families, and to provide protection to those who were not ready or willing to talk with the media. Army leadership wanted to help those who had risked themselves to help others to share their stories, but it was somewhat difficult to get them to talk. First, all available were busy in the post-Attack Pentagon, trying to restore offices, capabilities, and operations. We were also preparing for the far too many funerals and memorial ceremonies, and to remember and honor our fallen. Last, the Army is overall a reticent organization, and no one wanted or sought self-aggrandizement in this very troubling time.

On September 13, 2001, I was walking to my car to drive to Human Resources Command to help with training the call center staff when my cell phone rang. I answered and was surprised and delighted to hear the young female DCSPER PAO Captain on the line. She was alive and well. She had narrowly missed being killed, as she had decided to run a little longer that morning and was rushing back to her office when the plane hit the Pentagon. Unhurt, but knocked from her feet by the impact, she helped get injured to the hospital in the moments following the Attack. She did not realize she was on the "missing" list until earlier that day in a conversation with a colleague from DCSPERS. I remember the sense of relief I had learning she was safe. What a great phone call.

We did have to deal with and face losses in the aftermath of the attack. The Army's personnel system took the lead and death confirmation, and next-of-kin notifications were done, but there was a maddingly long period for the process to take. The DUSTWUN status for Army personnel is based in law, regulations and customs, but provides safeguards to ensure people are protected. Autopsies and DNA matching had to be done, and in some cases, the amount and comingling of remains made identification problematic.

Meanwhile, an interesting behavior developed within parts of the Pentagon workforce. Before the attack, the decorum was *very* professional and circumspect. The halls had been very quiet and polite; interactions between coworkers were tempered by the Clinton-era workplace harassment and propriety. Suddenly that reserve was replaced with greetings of, "*It's so good to see you!*" and hearty handshakes or hugs, often with tears of emotions post 9/11, especially when seeing someone for the first time since the Attack.

Camp Unity

"Camp Unity" in the Pentagon's South Parking lot. Image from Pentagon 9/11, DOD image, 2001

One of the results of the 9/11 Attack on the Pentagon was the disruption of basic services provided by vendors and staff for meals, haircuts and other routine services. The temporary and widespread smoke and water damage, combined with the electrical disruptions and enhanced security combined to limit access and services in the Building. Plus, who could or would want to eat sitting in a space saturated with the smoke and soot of a complex fire?

Camp Unity sprang to life with the first outreach from nearby businesses wanting to help and donate goods and services. It provided food, rest and support - a respite from search and recovery operations and welcomed Pentagon staff as well. For a brief period, Camp Unity provided meals and other support to the Pentagon staff.

In speaking with one of the Soldiers on guard outside the Pentagon, he told me that a semi-truck had slowly approached the Building late in the afternoon of September 11, and stopped. The passenger door opened, and a gent hopped down with a clipboard in hand and spoke with the guards. He said he had bottled water, sports drinks, shovels and brooms on the truck, and a large, big-box store nearby with flashlights, and other items. He asked where he could have the truck unloaded to help with the search and recovery effort, and what else was needed.

Others arrived as well, including a men's group from an Evangelical church in Tennessee. They had driven overnight and specialized in barbeque and smoked meats and asked where they could set up to feed people. A large poultry corporation sent a freezer trailer of frozen chicken and other meat, and others donated socks and underwear. The idea with that was searching the rubble of the Pentagon was hot, nasty work and at least changing into fresh underclothes and socks would make the work less burdensome.

Soon there was a veterinarian tent, checking and treating the search and security dogs in the recovery effort. A barber set up shop and gave free haircuts. The USO arrived and help to coordinate the space. Nationally-known, big-name hamburger chains had kiosks and competed to see who could give away more burgers and meals on a given day.

In the shadow of the Pentagon, for the month after the attack, Camp Unity was a positive pillar of community and normalcy that helped us heal and get back on our feet.

One of many heartfelt and impromptu memorials on the grounds at and near the Pentagon. DoD publication photo.

Dealing with Public Support – Life after the Pentagon

In a way it is ironic, as I never wanted the Pentagon assignment, but now I am linked to the Pentagon, regardless. The 9/11 Attacks also changed the arc of my military career. On September 10, 2001, I was planning on a career of "20 years and 20 minutes," the bare minimum to qualify for retirement. On 9/10, the Army was no longer fun, and the idea of rolling into a good-paying post-Army job was something desired. My Army goals and dreams had long been extinguished, and the post-Cold War Army was not too much to my liking. If I was going to do PR or lead others for a living, I wanted better conditions and better pay, or so I thought.

In the aftermath of 9/11, we were a nation and world attacked, and an Army at War. Priorities changed, attitudes changed, and people refocused on what our mission and our reason for serving was. As we recovered from the Attack, honored, and buried our dead, I had to tell my spouse and family that reality had changed. I was in the Army, and we were at war. That was my priority. My retirement would have to wait.

I still had to finish my Pentagon assignment, which ran through June 2003. Even with the changes – wearing our BDUs (combat fatigues) as our daily uniform, and handling issues with deployments to Afghanistan and later Iraq, the Pentagon was still a major coordination and policy headquarter, making high-level decisions about Army-wide policies, not the tactical or operational matters of fighting the war on terror. I was promoted to Lt. Col. on Oct. 1, 2001, after having been selected for promotion prior to the Attack.

I volunteered to open Army Public Affairs Chicago in late 2002, following the 1st Anniversary of 9/11. Based on my time in the Midwest as a college student at Mizzou, and teaching ROTC in Minnesota, combined with my previous assignments in New York and elsewhere, I felt I was a great choice to stand up and open the Army's outreach and marketing office in Chicago. In early 2003, my family and I moved just northwest of Chicago, and I started that next chapter.

In many ways, opening the Army's Midwest office was an ideal assignment for me. I would be "away from the flagpole" and on my own, creating something new, telling the Army story and connecting and networking. But I was also the "Pentagon guy" who had survived the 9/11 Attack. People would ask about it, and I was deft at changing the topic and staying light, until I was not.

In April 2003, I spoke at a luncheon of business and community leaders at the Union League Club of Chicago. The topic was *The Army At War and Transforming*, which was the main communication effort that Army leadership wanted to be shared with key audiences. The talk had gone reasonably well, until we got to the questions and answers. After some polite questions, I was asked, "So, what was it like for you in the Pentagon on 9/11? What did you do?"

I blubbered, stammered, and choked up in my response. With more emotion than I cared for, I shared with them the pride I felt. Not of what I had done, but what I had witnessed. The bravery and service of others. The challenges faced and overcome. Embarrassed that I had broken down and cried in front of so many people, I was not ready for their support or acceptance, but was grateful for their applause. Later, a decorated Vietnam veteran who was in the audience, told me to consider getting some help for PTSD. He saw it in me.

That was the start of my talking in public about what I witnessed, did, and contributed in the Pentagon on 9/11.

Since then, I have done well over a thousand talks, speeches and presentations about 9/11, and have sought to share what I witnessed and did. Over time, talking about the Attacks has helped me heal, and I hope has helped others. With about 20,000 Pentagon survivors, and a couple hundred who did something other than evacuating the building and going home, I think my account is unique, and in the Midwest, I am one of the few.

The Army Staff Identification Badge (ASIB) is not an award or decoration, but a mark of service at Headquarters Department of the Army (HQDA) for more than a year. They are visible signs of professional growth associated with the important duties and responsibilities of the Army Secretariat and the Army Staff (ARSTAF). Issuance is not automatic but is based on demonstrated outstanding performance of duty and approval by a principal HQDA official. The black silk mourning ribbon was my unofficial way of noting my Pentagon assignment. I suggested this as a simple way for Army Staff 9/11 Attack survivors to be recognized, but since not all Army personnel present on 9/11 would be eligible for the ASIB, it was not practical. Ironically, my ASIB certificate is dated September 11, 2001, and was on my boss' desk that day, waiting for a good time for it to be presented.

Originally commissioned on September 11, 2001, the Pentagon Memorial Service Coin, designed by C. Forbes Inc., was presented to Army Pentagon staff in October 2001. There was also a matching lapel pin presented at the Memorial Service. This coin is 1 3/4" Nickel Silver finish, with a high-quality die-struck heavy metal alloy and hand-painted color enamel fill. Challenge Coins are a military tradition.

9/11 SURVIVORS' STORIES

DEPARTMENT OF THE ARMY

THIS IS TO CERTIFY THAT THE SECRETARY OF THE ARMY HAS AWARDED

THE ARMY COMMENDATION MEDAL

TO LIEUTENANT COLONEL TIMOTHY R. YANTIS
OFFICE OF THE CHIEF OF STAFF, PUBLIC AFFAIRS

FOR meritorious achievement after a hijacked aircraft was used by terrorists as a weapon to attack the Pentagon. Lieutenant Colonel Yantis sought out the wounded and moved from triage point to triage point to render assistance. He disregarded orders to evacuate for his own safety, secured additional medical supplies, helped organize relief efforts and acted with steadfast purpose and courage for many hours. Lieutenant Colonel Yantis' actions are in keeping with the finest traditions of military service and reflect great credit upon himself and the United States Army.

11 SEPTEMBER 2001

THIS 13TH DAY OF MARCH 2002

Permanent Order 072-26
United States Army Personnel Command
Alexandria, Virginia 22332-0471

THE ADJUTANT GENERAL

INTERN AT THE PENTAGON

by Trisha Shaffer-Papantonakis

September 11, 2001...in some ways it feels like yesterday, in other ways it feels like somebody else's lifetime ago. The sky was an incredible blue and the clouds looked like something from an animated movie; they were so perfect. The weather was just right, too, I thought as I walked to the metro station. I was excited. I was 19 years old, a junior enrolled at Mount Vernon Nazarene University in Mount Vernon, Ohio. Although I was studying for a double bachelor's degree in psychology and sociology/criminal justice, I also had a strong background in journalism. I had been my high school yearbook editor for two years and had just finished editing my college yearbook for my sophomore year. It was the second day of my Council of Christian Colleges and Universities (CCCU) American Studies Program (ASP) internship. The ASP couldn't find a placement for me with a criminal justice focus, but they were able to find a place for me with the Army Office of Public Affairs. I was going to learn so much about the way a public affairs department worked. I had met a most of the people I was going to be working for the day before, but on 9/11, I was going to learn what my main project would be for the duration of my semester with the Army Office of Public Affairs.

I arrived at the Pentagon Metro Station and as I stepped off the tram, I noticed the Pentagon's large internal Metro station. Anyone was able to exit the train at the stop; however, people had to pass security in order to completely enter the Pentagon. People with Pentagon credentials were able to scan through a turnstile and walk right in. Since I did not have my official ID yet, I had to wait for someone to bring me up the office. Nothing seemed out of place; little did I know this would be the last time I would be inside this station. After about 20 minutes, a Captain from my new team met me and said that an airplane had hit one of the Twin Towers in New York and to be prepared because we were in for a long day. "Kamikaze?" I asked. I could not believe what I was hearing; it had to be an accident. No one would attack Americans on our soil! "Yes," was her simple reply.

We made our way in silence to the office, which was in the process of being packed away; we would be moving into the recently remodeled area within a matter of weeks. While the officers wore their dress uniforms, civilians, like myself, were expected to wear office attire. I felt especially cute that morning in my pale blue blouse, which perfectly matched the oversized flowers on my knee-length skirt. I sat down at my desk, took off my tennis shoes, and slipped on my black heels. "I shouldn't have skipped breakfast!" I thought to myself. My nerves, combined with my tendency for running late, caused me to skip breakfast to ensure I would arrive to my internship on time. The Pentagon had plenty of food options, from coffee and bagel shops to a sit-down, buffet-style cafeteria. Though it housed a multitude of offices, the building was designed so that no two rooms were more than a 15-minute walk apart. Although the bagel shop was just around the corner, I didn't have clearance to walk there unescorted.

As I stood to ask if someone could chaperone me, there was a loud "BOOM!" The building shook. I sat back down in shock; one of the air compressors from the construction crew must have exploded, I thought. I looked into the hallway and saw that people were flowing out from where the initial sound had originated, and smoke was filling the ceiling. The people evacuating were controlled and orderly, yet the seriousness of what had just happened could be felt. The continuous loud, low rumbling and the number of people evacuating meant this had to be more than an air compressor explosion--much more. Next thing I knew, a gentleman poked his head in the door and told us all to evacuate; he turned out to be Nancy's (my official supervisor) husband. I grabbed my purse and cell phone and followed Nancy and her husband out; I had no idea where we were going.

As we briskly walked through the corridor to the emergency exit, I asked Nancy if this happened often. She half laughed and said in her 20-plus years there, they had only been evacuated once before, for a bomb threat. I followed them out of the building and through the grassy areas around the Pentagon. More and more people poured into the lawn with us. It was hard to believe that so many people had fit in the building--and we were in only one of five sides. I saw people injured and bleeding, but no one was there to help them. Anyone with any medical or emergency training was tending to the people at the impact site, taking care of people in much worse condition. I wanted to stop and help, but I was just a college intern and not trained in emergencies.

Huge chunks of building lay in the middle of the street. As we continued to walk, I turned to see the impact site. Smoke billowed out of a building that just the day before had been a functional monument to the strength of our nation. It seemed as though we walked forever. My feet began hurting from walking in heels. We were hearing rumors that a second plane hit the WTC, another plane hit the White House, and yet another was headed for the other side of the Pentagon. Time became blurred. Minutes felt like hours, hours like minutes. Someone suggested to move everyone to a tree-covered area; standing in an open parking lot seemed like we were making ourselves a target. It was then I started realizing the gravity of what just happened. I tried calling my mom, but the lines were all busy.

Meanwhile, back in Ohio, my mom was at work. A close friend of hers told her that a plane had hit the World Trade Center, and my mom's response was that I was safe inside the Pentagon. No sooner had she said that than the sales manager, who knew I was interning, said, "Brenda, they hit the Pentagon." My mother fell to her knees and prayed as she called my college. The lady on the phone began praying for my mother, as the area the plane hit was where our offices were moving, and she believed I had been in the direct line of the plane. The woman promised she would call my mom as soon as they heard any news. My mom continued to pray for my protection.

My dad was an over-the-road trucker. He was blissfully unaware that anything had happened that morning, until he saw the massive amount of missed calls on his phone. Finally, he called his brother back and learned what had happened. My father hung up with his brother and dialed my number.

The phone lines were down, so I had no way of letting my family or my school know I was okay. By now we had received the all-clear and were told to make our way home and wait for instructions. I did not have a car, and the Pentagon Metro had been destroyed in the blast, so Nancy had said she would give me a ride back to my apartment in D.C. As we were pulling out of the parking spot, my phone rang; it was my father! I quickly told him that I was okay; shaken up but uninjured. I asked him to call my mom and my school and relay the message. We got off the phone quickly to free up the lines for someone else.

Driving towards D.C., we realized that the government had shut down the city to vehicles. My best choice to get to my apartment was the subway. We found an open station and I figured out how I could get back home, bypassing the destroyed Pentagon terminal. As I walked onto the empty train car, I could not contain the tears any longer. The ride was quiet, but soon, the conductor came on and said that the Metro had been ordered to stop. The next station would be the closest he could get me to my apartment. I walked out of the subway and once again saw the beautiful sky. How could the sky still be so beautiful on such a horrible day? I was miles from my apartment, but was thankful for the logical layout of D.C. or I would have been horribly lost! It felt like I was the only one in the city; the streets were so empty. My feet were killing me and I took my shoes off. Finally, at 7 p.m., I made it back to my apartment and my internship host.

The next day I was finally able to talk to my mother. She wanted me to come home, but I told her, "NO!" I was most certainly NOT going home. I also had to convince my fiancé, who had driven to my mom's house with the intention of picking her up to head out to Washington and get me. What they didn't understand was that in my mind, if I went home, then the terrorists would win. I was not about to let that happen. I could not fight in a war. I could not help those poor injured people, but I could show up for work when they called me back in.

In the days that followed, we had meetings on the American Studies Program Campus. Some of my fellow students wanted to pack up and go back home. Looking back, I did not realize at the time that the events of 9/11 traumatized our entire country. All I could think about was that they hadn't seen the things I saw. Acute post-traumatic stress disorder distorted my thinking, and, in those moments, I could only barely process the trauma I had just been through. I became angry with these students and said things I shouldn't have said, I wish I could go back apologize to my ASP classmates.

I did not want to go home, but I did want to leave Washington, D.C. I booked myself a train ticket and headed up to Baltimore, Maryland, and spend the weekend with my fiancé's father and his family.

On Monday morning, I returned from Baltimore and went directly to the Pentagon. I had my weekend bag with me. President George W. Bush was at the Pentagon, and I walked right into the path they had set up for his tour. Security was completely different. My bag had been checked, yet, I watched as Secret Service agents noticed me with my bag and diverted the President away from me.

I was shown to my new office, as I still did not have clearance to walk the Pentagon alone. I was completely uncertain of what I'd be doing and soon found that everything had changed. Instead of filing and simple clerical work, soon I was answering media calls and taking messages for the other staff members. Because of this, I ended up working more with Lieutenant Colonel Ryan Yantis. Because our old office had received smoke and fire damage, we were displaced. We were not allowed back into the original offices for weeks. Even when we were granted one trip, there were limits on what we could bring back. If it was fabric, it had to be washed separately from our other clothing before wearing. Any other items had to be wiped down due to asbestos and smoke contamination.

There were 12 of us working from five desks, answering thousands of media calls out of a temporary office that felt more like a coat closet. We became family, battle buddies. In the times that my name would slip LTC Yantis' mind, I became "Blonde Girl." And I was…but I did a lot of growing up. The things I thought were important just a few days earlier became nothing to me as I watched my new friends discover that some of their longtime friends hadn't survived the attack. A few weeks later, I experienced the joy our officed shared when one of our co-workers gave birth. I learned that when people share a goal, they can overcome just about anything.

About a month after the attacks, I received a call from a reporter requesting an interview from a soldier whose husband was a Navy officer who had been killed at the Pentagon. I knew the soldier had already denied interviews and was not interested. The reporter was upset when I told him the interview was not possible and he became angry, saying it had already been a month! I replied that "while we are going home to our families, she is going home to an empty house every day for the past month." The caller became irate with me and asked to speak to my supervisor. I turned to find LTC Yantis standing behind me and I handed the phone to him. Without skipping a beat, he told the reporter that he had heard every word of our conversation and that he would not be granted an interview with that soldier now, or ever. "Good job, Blonde Girl," LTC Yantis said.

My internship was over in December. By the time I left, we had moved the office into a newer, larger space. Although I had only worked a few months with these people, it felt as though I had known them forever. I miss the comradery we shared during those months as "battle buddies". I went my separate way and, eventually, they all did too. I graduated from Mount Vernon Nazarene University in May of 2003 with a double bachelor's degree in psychology and sociology: criminal justice track.

In October 2003, I married the love of my life and became Trisha Papantonakis. In 2005 and 2007, we were blessed with two amazing daughters, Kadence and Evnomia. In 2011 we had our son, Rhyan. 2013 brought our final daughter, Aurora. Our family became complete when in 2017, we became parents to our youngest, Zayden.

After years of being a stay-at-home mom, in 2009, my family and I opened a Once Upon A Child franchise in Niles, Ohio. While I enjoy helping our community find affordable, gently-used children's items, I still felt a pull and a passion to enter healthcare. So, at the age of 39, I returned to school to pursue a nursing degree and will graduate with my Bachelor of Science degree in nursing in 2024--the same year as my oldest daughter graduates high school! I still feel a small degree of survivor's guilt. As a nurse, I will be able to care for people in a way I was unable to do on 9/11.

With the advent of Facebook, I was able to reconnect with some of my Battle Buddies. In 2010, while expecting my third child, I read about the actions of LTC Yantis on 9/11. I discovered that while I was being led away, he was pulling people from the destruction. He was saving lives. Shortly after the 10th anniversary of 9/11, my son was born, and I could not think of a better name for him. If you ask my son, Rhyan, who he is named after, he answers "my mom's hero". LTC Ryan Yantis helped me feel like a true part of the Army Public Affairs team, not just some nameless college intern. Without him, I would feel as though that part of my life had actually happened to someone else. I will forever hold the cherished moniker of "Blonde Girl" close to my heart and, in fact, have fondly nicknamed by daughter, Evnomia, "Blonde Girl".

TICKET TO A MEMORIAL

by Thomas R. Van Cleave

I am a travel agent and have owned Windmill City Travel in Batavia, Illinois, since 1981. My company focused on incentive travel for businesses and providing rewards for loyal customers and sales staff. September, 2001, was a typical, good month; I had a number of business clients traveling to various destinations around the country. My older daughter was spending the semester studying abroad in Paris, France. My wife, an American Airlines flight attendant, had been able to travel to Paris to join our daughter to celebrate her birthday, which was September 11th.

On the beautiful morning of 9/11, I was planning to call my wife and daughter to wish my daughter a happy birthday, when the day's plans drastically changed. I was still at home drinking my morning coffee, when I saw on TV the first news of an airplane hitting the World Trade Center (WTC). I thought it was a small, misguided private airplane that had flown into the tower. Regardless of the cause, I hurried to my office because I knew my clients travel plans would be disrupted. When I got there, the second tower had been hit. I learned that all flights were grounded and told to land immediately wherever they were. My first thought was to be thankful that my wife was not in the air. I wanted to contact my wife and daughter in Paris, but I was unable to reach them. I knew that my wife was a savvy traveler and would call as soon as she was able.

Within moments, the phone started ringing with stranded clients scattered all over the United States. I soon discovered car rentals were sold out in all the major airports. I called a colleague to ask what she was doing for her clients, and she said that she was referring clients to U-Haul truck rental. The advice worked; many of my clients were able to get home by renting a truck one-way. I was beginning to feel relieved that I had taken care of most of my clients.

As the day progressed and desperate phone calls slowed, I was able to feel relieved that I had taken care of most of my clients; most were safe and able to make a plan to get back to Chicago. I was even more relieved when I heard from my wife and daughter, who were finally able to call the U.S. They heard of the attacks from a pharmacist who recognized them as American and suggested they return to their hotel to call loved ones. He invited them to watch the news that was on his television, so they could see the magnitude of this attack. They immediately returned to their hotel and were able to call me. Hearing their voices put me at ease that they were okay.

On September 13th, limited flights began. On the 14th, I received a call from a lady who desperately wanted a round-trip ticket to Boston in two days. I advised her it would be very expensive because of the limitations on flights and asked her why it was so important for her to get to Boston. Was it a business trip? She said, "No, I need to attend the memorial service in Boston for the American Airlines flight crew that had been aboard the plane that crashed into the World Trade Center."

I said to her, "You can't just fly to Boston to attend the memorial service unless you have an invitation."

She said, "My son was one of the crew members on the Boston flight that crashed into the tower."

Then I said to her, "American Airlines is providing transportation for the family members. Call American Airlines."

She responded, "American Airlines is providing 8 tickets per crew member for family to attend the service. My ex-husband's family already took the 8 tickets. There are no more tickets available for me."

I was amazed by that statement. I couldn't imagine that the ex-husband would not invite his son's mother to the memorial. I knew that there was a memorial service scheduled in two days at the American Airlines hangar at Boston's Logan Field. I asked for her name and if she could verify that she is the birth mother of the crew member. His mother said she lived in the adjoining town, and the information could be verified. She then made the statement, "Don't ever disown one of your children. My son was gay, and I was not able to accept it. When I disowned him, he and the rest of the family cut me out."

Now I understood why the family had not made a ticket available to her.

Since my wife is an AA flight attendant, I had an emergency contact number for her supervisor. I could use this number if I need to contact her in case of an emergency at home while she is working a flight. I called the number at O'Hare and explained the situation involving the crew member's mother. The supervisor said she would pass on the information to the appropriate person. Within two hours, I got a call from American Airlines in Chicago, stating that a person in Boston who was coordinating the memorial service would call me. Within a couple hours, I got a call from the gentleman who was coordinating the service in Boston, and he took all the mother's information. He called me the next day to tell me that the mother was booked on a flight to Boston the following day and that an American Airlines representative would meet her in Boston.

I relayed this information to the mother, and she was amazed that I had been able to help her. She had called eight other travel agencies and no one else had been able to help. By the way, she added, she was so upset over the loss of her son that she needed some emotional support from a friend to make the trip with her. Could I get her a ticked for her best friend to join her?

My first thought was, *why didn't you ask me that sooner*, but I told myself to calm down and I called the coordinator in Boston. The airline kindly provided the ticket.

I was relieved to be of help, even though I was aware that it might be an awkward situation.

Two months after the attack, the American Society of Travel Agents (ASTA), held their annual convention in New York City. The meeting was originally scheduled for Seville, Spain, but was quickly rearranged for New York. ASTA felt it was important for the travel agent community to support the hotels and tourist attractions in NYC. This move gave the city over 9,000 room nights of revenue. As an ASTA member, I attended the convention and had the opportunity to walk around the terrible crash site. It was barricaded, but there were peep holes in the fences that allowed some viewing. Two months after 9/11, a red glow was still visible in the center of the site and smoke was still billowing over the area. The streets were filled with white ash, and I remember looking into a small card shop where the racks of cards were blown over and scattered all over the store. The windows were all blown out and nothing had been touched inside the store since the attack. I was reminded of the terror of the day and of the horror and pain suffered by so many victims and their families. I finally fully understood the desperation of the mother wanting to share in the memorial to her son.

My wife retired after 44 years of flying International from American Airlines and has never desired to go inside the 9/11 museum at the WTC site. She has walked the "Wall of Names" and stops for a prayer for the souls of the crew members and all the other innocent souls.

As time passed, I had put aside the mother's statements, although I had long remembered the pain and grief that had been caused by her treatment of her son. Life lessons are delivered in many ways--listen to them. Having loved ones who identify with the LGBTQ+ community, our acceptance and love of them was the same on September 10, 2001, as it is today. However, the call on September 14th reminded me that not all families are the same and that tragedy can bring perspective, although in this instance, too late. I share this story in the hopes that someone who needs to hear it is in the process of repairing a relationship that may be in disrepair: to save someone from the pain of learning an all too important lesson after it is too late.

In August 2019 it was my family's honor to watch as my son marry the love of his life, Jon. It was a joy that the woman I spoke to could have been able to be a part of, if and when her son would have married; he did have a significate partner and they lived in California. I will never know the pain of losing an estranged child and I hope others will not either. If anyone is experiencing estrangement, I hope that you pursue reconciliation, even if it means putting aside your beliefs to honor reality. I've heard what the most profound regret sounds like, and I hope that no one ever has to feel it again.

UNION LEAGUE CLUB OF CHICAGO

by Ryan Yantis

With Chicago being one hour behind the east coast cities and sites where the 9/11 Attacks were unfolding, the news reached the city in the heights of the morning rush hour. Chicago is a commuter city, especially in the Loop – the financial and business capitol of the Midwest – with hundreds of thousand commuters daily, plus visiting business travelers and tourist. The news of the 9/11 Attacks, combined with the realization and potential for a local attack against the Sears Tower (since renamed to the Willis Tower), led to an immediate voluntary and government-suggested evacuation and reverse commute of a large number of people out of the city.

The METRA train system packed trains to capacity, and Chicago Transit Authority train and busses moved quickly, giving the Loop areas of Chicago what some termed an eerie, post-apocalyptic feel. Street that normally teemed with people on a workday were wholly deserted. Streets normally choked with cars, taxis, busses and pedestrians were empty, save for loose trash and dropped papers rustling in the breeze. September 11, 2001 was a beautiful day in Chicago as well, warm with light clouds, and empty streets. Following FAA and federal government orders, all the major airports in the region and across the Midwest shut down after landing and securing all the aircraft that were flying that morning.

But there were business travelers and tourists. They were in hotels, motels, and in cases, private clubs across the country and Chicago. One of those clubs was the Union League Club of Chicago (ULCC). The ULCC also provided support and assistance to the 9/11 Chicagoland Survivors.

A private club, the ULCC has its roots going back to the American Civil War. Founded in early 1863, the ULCC sought to support the Union and the American government against the Confederacy. The club helped to raise military units to fight in the Union Army, worked against secessionist efforts and tendencies in the Midwest. The ULCC was part of a larger network of similar clubs, with *Union League* across the country in Boston, New York City, Philadelphia, and other smaller cities. Through dynamic membership, the ULCC seeks to support action in nonpartisan political, economic and social arenas, with important interests on social issues including justice, education, and good government.

With areas devoted to meeting rooms, libraries, dining and social activities, and other pleasant activities, the ULCC also had guest rooms for business travelers or members. Think of plush, well-appointed hotel rooms with all the amenities, but with rates comparable to less distinguished settings.

From the ULCC website:

The ULCC is everything a private club should be and more. The Clubhouse facilities include two restaurants, a gastro pub, a coffee shop, event spaces that seat from two to 400, six floors of fitness facilities, large and small conference rooms, a library, remote workspaces, and 180 overnight guest rooms. The Union League Club is rated one of the top private clubs in the country.

On the afternoon of September 11, 2001, the Club's manager on duty (MOD) was struggling to balance the needs of the club's staff, with the more than 80 business travelers and tourists now effectively stranded by the closing of US airspace and travel restrictions. Many of the staff were ready to head home after a long and stressful day, and the evening shift had not come in as planned, due to commute difficulties and personal reasons. There was a Club to run, guests to feed and care for, and the day-to-day operations that needed to continue.

The MOD gathered the staff available and talked with them. He knew his staff were only human – they were tired, unsettled by the events of the day, and they wanted to go home. But there were guests in the club. These guests were effectively stranded, waiting to see what September 12th would bring. The manager asked the staff to consider these guests against their own interests and needs, and that the club needed to care for these people. With one or two exceptions – people with childcare challenges – the staff remained on duty and at their posts to care for others.

Compounding this was the central location of the ULCC, with two huge federal office buildings, including federal courtrooms, being immediately adjacent. To the west on Jackson Boulevard is the Ralph H. Metcalfe Federal Building (28 stories), with the Kluczynski Federal Building (45 stories) being across Jackson to the north. Just to the west of the ULCC on Jackson was the Chicago Board of Trade building, the Federal Reserve Bank – Chicago, and many major business offices and buildings.

(Related to Ryan in a conversation with Howard, the MOD, in April 2003 during one of my first visits to the ULCC)

The club also assisted the Chicagoland 9/11 Survivors with a meeting room – including food and drink in 2005 – 2007. Monthly meeting of the Survivors with Willow House staff and counselors had become a challenge. With most of the Chicagoland area Survivors living in distant suburbs, including northern Indiana, getting to and home from the evening meetings was a challenge. When asked if they would support the meetings with a room, the club, in the heart of the Loop, stepped forward and met that need. This gave the Survivors who worked in the Loop the opportunity to meet, get the support needed, and to still have time with family and sleep.

The club also led and supported efforts to remember the losses and honor those still suffering in Annual Remembrance ceremonies and other public events. The club hosted and supported annual 9/11 ceremonies and other events.

In many ways, the ULCC represented what many survivors found throughout the Midwest. Good people, leaning forward and trying to help others in the rough times after 9/11. The many community groups, clubs, and non-profits that stepped up to help first responders, military members and veterans was very impressive.

WILLOW HOUSE

Chicago area

"What can you do for us?" asked 9/11 Attack survivor, Joe Dittmar. That fundamental question forged a new chapter in Willow House's history; we had to learn how to be the helpers for these heroic individuals. Here's our story.

Stefanie Norris, MSL, LCSW

I'm Stefanie Norris, MSW, LCSW and founder of Willow House, a non-profit organization dedicated to developing and providing free supportive services for children, teens and young adults and their families coping with grief and the death of a parent, sibling or child. The morning of September 11, 2001, I, along with most of our country, was riveted to news coverage of the frightening attacks on the World Trade Center. I was stunned, frightened and in disbelief. As the reality of this attack set in, I was overwhelmed with very personal and extreme worry for my extended family and friends. who lived mostly in New York and in the tri-state area--many of whom worked in the city at the time. I was aware of the extreme danger and risk that many I love were likely in, and I was afraid and helpless to do anything for them. My calls to the area didn't go through; I had no idea if anyone had been injured, or worse.

With my professional background in clinical social work, and specialty in death and grief, I feared the worst for so many and imagined that most had, at the very least, been traumatized. I settled in for the long day, awaiting news. As we learned of the attack on the Pentagon and the hijacking of Flight 93, which ultimately crashed in Pennsylvania, the magnitude of deaths and grief and trauma grew and grew, with the media considering the potential of many thousands of deaths.

Specializing in work supporting grieving children and families, I was overwhelmed with wondering how an unimaginable number of children and families would be helped, supported and counselled? At some point that day, or possibly later, I reached out to a colleague and we discussed how we could find support for so many grieving children. We were in the midst of developing a national organization (what is now the National Alliance for Grieving Children [NAGC]) to increase these unique supportive services for children nationwide.

After those first few weeks and months beyond the 9/11 Attacks, we learned of growing and newly developed support services in the tri-states area. Programs across the country, like Willow House, wondered how to help the victims, survivors, and grieving children and families. We had to learn new skills quickly; we were the helpers.

We also knew we had to remain committed to our Willow House children and families who were not affected by 9/11, while continuing to reach out to the 9/11 children and families who were in serious crisis.

Our team reached out to a New York program similar to Willow House. We let them know that Willow House children and teens wanted to offer support to their peers and wanted to send letters, messages and drawings to youth members who were in crisis due to 9/11, if they would be agreeable to receiving them. They were agreeable and grateful, and, as we expected, Willow House children benefitted from knowing they contributed to their new bereaved "friends" in New York. The children shared their condolences, thoughts, experiences and wisdom about grieving and losing a mom, dad, sibling or other loved one. Their messages included many hearts, rainbows, flowers, poems and other symbols and words that expressed hope. We didn't know at the time that this was actually the start of Willow House providing support for those most horrifically affected by 9/11, the courageous survivors who were residing in the Midwest.

We had worked with the Chicago FBI Victims Assistance team a few times beginning in 1999, when Northwestern University's Coach Ricky Birdsong was shot and killed while jogging in his own neighborhood with his two children, who were just eight and 10 years old. A man, later identified as a "white supremacist," continued on a shooting spree, injuring six men and killing a college student. With the assistance of the FBI, Willow House was able to provide support to the small neighborhood of children and families where Coach Birdsong had lived and died, and to the families of others injured and traumatized by these events. Therefore, I was not completely surprised when the Chicago FBI called and asked us to meet with Chicago-area 9/11 families they had identified, and to whom they were providing victims' assistance.

The agents were especially sensitive to the depth of grief, loss and fears these families were enduring, and asked us to provide emotional and grief support for their first in-person meeting of 9/11 families. After that first meeting with some of the Midwestern families, they were all receptive to our offer to provide ongoing support through support groups and referrals, as needed, for additional assistance.

Three years later, as we continued the 9/11 support groups, we heard from Joe Dittmar.

Kirsten Belzer, LCSW, CHT

My name is Kirsten Belzer, LCSW, CHT and former project director of the Willow House 9/11 survivors' support group. I learned a great deal personally and professionally in this role and will always be indebted to Willow House and the survivors for the opportunity to be a part of their healing journeys. These were businesspeople and members of the military who were willing to be vulnerable, share tears and open their hearts, trying to find ways of healing themselves and others. It was an incredible honor and privilege to work with such dedicated, heroic, generous people and to watch their resiliency through the process. This experience greatly impacted my own psychotherapy practice, as I now incorporated eye movement desensitization and reprocessing therapy (EMDR Therapy), and other trauma treatment lessons, into what I do with anyone who has experienced trauma. I often think of the 9/11 survivors and their spirit of generosity in wanting to help others, and I know that what I learned in working with them has greatly assisted me in helping many people with all sorts of trauma.

One key element of trauma I learned, was that survivors have instincts others may not. For instance, they are more likely to survive subsequent traumas. One hero of the day was a middle-aged man who had experienced other life-threatening experiences in his earlier life. Despite being told on the loudspeaker to stay where he was after the first plane hit, he knew he needed to get out of his building and took a disabled woman in a wheelchair with him. Within moments of their escape, the second plane hit his building. He and the woman would have surely perished, based on the location of their office, had he not followed his instincts, most likely developed from past near-death encounters.

Every day, each of us makes more decisions than we can

count. Should I stop for coffee and potentially miss the train? Go to that meeting? Tie my shoelace right now? Leave the building that hasn't yet been hit by a plane, despite being told by officials that I need to stay in place? For the survivors of 9/11, even one of those decisions could have meant the difference between life and death. It makes sense that many survivors of 9/11 would walk away ruminating about what may or may not have been.

Together, Stefanie and I will tell the story of Willow House's journey in helping 9/11 survivors in the greater Chicagoland area heal from their enormously traumatic experiences. It is an honor for us both to have had the opportunity to know each individual who has bravely shared story in this book.

9/11 Survivors' Support Group

Willow House's contact with the 9/11 survivors began with a phone call after Stefanie Norris, founder and then executive director, spoke on a radio segment. A survivor, Joe Dittmar, called to say he appreciated hearing the interview about how Willow House was serving the 9/11 bereaved families, but he asked, "What can you do for us?" For three years, those who had escaped the Pentagon and World Trade Center dealt with trauma reactions, yet there was no formal support for them in the Midwest.

The 9/11 survivors who attended Willow House groups experienced unimaginably frightening attacks and the deaths of thousands amidst the massive destruction. Climbing down the stairs of the World Trade Center's Towers, some came face-to-face with unforgettable heroic rescuers climbing upstairs to help others, but who would not climb back down, perishing within the towers. Their faces, their eyes, their heroism, will never be forgotten by these survivors.

These 9/11 survivors were grieving. Their lives had been shaken and they were forever changed, as they were finding their way to their "new normal". Many were isolated with their 9/11 experience in the Midwest, away from the attack sites and thousands of survivors on the East Coast. All were anxious and looking forward to coming together to experience "support" as a group.

Some survivors experienced anxiety, depression and traumatic reactions, triggering sensory trauma, post-traumatic stress disorder, survivors' guilt, and more. When Willow House began to prepare to provide support services for 9/11 survivors, the clinical team had already had three years of experience with 9/11 family members who lost a loved one in the attacks, and some understanding of the survivors' experiences.

Willow House had always focused on the bereaved. However, this was a new challenge for the organization. Stefanie reached out to the mental health professionals and trauma experts on the East Coast to ask how they were helping survivors there. Most replied that in their experience a type of trauma therapy, called eye movement desensitization and reprocessing therapy (EMDR), was effective at providing relief. EMDR uses bilateral stimulation of the brain to reprocess trauma memories to calm the nervous system and elicit an adaptive response. This is accomplished through moving the eyes back and forth or tapping the right and left side of the body, to use both sides of the brain to help clear out the distress from trauma.

While it may sound unorthodox, more than 30 randomized clinical studies have established the effectiveness of EMDR, and the Veterans Administration recommends it as one of the top trauma therapies for post-traumatic stress disorder. 9/11 Project Director Kirsten Belzer, LCSW, arranged for the EMDR Humanitarian Assistance Program (HAP) to facilitate an EMDR three-day training and invited 12 other non-profit organizations to join in receiving this specialized training. Two months later, the group attended the second level of training presented by EMDR-HAP.

Willow House began offering groups for survivors, as well as individual therapy using EMDR therapy for those who experienced post-traumatic stress disorder. The connections forged in group between the members seemed meaningful after the three years of trying to cope alone with their traumas. Eventually, Willow House was in contact with 13 survivors in the Midwest. Some of the focus on the groups was to provide psychoeducation about trauma reactions, to help normalize what each was experiencing.

Willow House provided each survivor with an educational packet about trauma and a book, *Invisible Heroes: Survivors of Trauma and How They Heal*, by Belleruth Naparstek, which discusses how the nervous system responds to trauma and ways to calm it, including using guided imagery, which is a form of meditation. The Willow House team provided education about how trauma is first a physiological response and second a psychological one. Kirsten provided guided imagery exercises in both group and individual therapy. Kirsten also provided hypnotherapy for smoking cessation for one survivor who began smoking after the attack; it was a joy for her to learn that he still wasn't smoking 15 years later.

The Survivors group had a great deal of energy and seemed to feel relieved to be together with others who could understand everyday reactions that often left them feeling crazy. For instance, the smell of a construction site or the sounds of the Chicago Air and Water show could immediately bring them back to the trauma of 9/11. The Willow House team was able to validate and normalize the survivors' experiences and help them understand that our nervous systems react in these ways to help protect us.

For example, smell brings back a felt sense of a past trauma the fastest of all the five senses. Our bodies have ways to try to protect us from future traumas by helping us sense danger. Unfortunately, this often spills into situations that may be similar in some way, such as the smell of a demolished building at a construction site, but not dangerous. The group members seemed to feel reassured that others were having similar experiences. These survivors were willing and able to connect and affirm each other and their experiences. Together, they created a sense of community, which helped in their resilience.

It is important to note according to the American Psychological Association, resiliency is: *"the process of adapting well* in the face of adversity, trauma, tragedy, threats, or significant sources of stress—such as family and relationship problems, serious health problems, or workplace and financial stressors. As much as resilience involves "bouncing back" from these difficult experiences, *it can also involve profound personal growth."*

Willow House's 9/11 Support Groups for families and survivors continued for more than five years. Throughout that time, the organization heard regularly from FBI Victim Assistance agents inquiring as to how families and survivors were doing and whether there was anything they could do to help.

Much like the survivors we were helping, the Willow House team, too, was functioning outside of the 9/11 community in New York City and Washington, D.C. Also, much like our survivors, we reached out to our peer "helpers" to learn and collaborate, so that we could continue to effectively help the Midwest survivors' community.

After five years, when our services began to wind down, one of the organizations that gave us the most financial support to help survivors, The Robin Hood Foundation, invited the Willow House team to a special event in New York City. The event honored organizations that provided programs and services to 9/11 families, survivors, first responders and others.

The room was filled with people whose clinical skills, integrity and powerful commitment to help those most affected by 9/11 move on to a spirit of resilience, growth and hope. For the first time, our team felt that we were, in fact, part of a larger team of "helpers" – greater than any one of our organizations, and greater than any one of those who rose to the occasion to ask for help. We all felt proud to have belonged to a remarkable gathering of "helpers" from all different corners of experience and geographic locations.

Today, the Midwest survivors remain a "community" of their own. They found one another, shared their experiences, their feelings, their challenges and frustrations. They shared their pain, their resilience, their heroism, their profound grief and their hope. They defined their "new normal," while supporting one another. The Willow House team helped them to normalize their many shared experiences, honoring one another's courage by clasping hands, sharing hugs and yes, sometimes flat out laughing. Often, laughing, in fact.

These survivors experienced the profound power and value of their own support group community. They were no longer isolated in their experience. Their community even had a name: the "Willow House 9/11 Survivors Group". The Willow House team was honored to facilitate these support group experiences and opportunities. Yet, the survivors did the hard work, opening up to understand and embrace one another, solidifying their community.

Just as all Willow House groups are intended for bereaved families, for the survivors, the community of a support group was an experience of normalizing and affirming shared experiences, and so much more that they found to be valuable on their journey to healing. One final concept we'd like to share is that of post-traumatic growth, which we saw in all who participated in our 9/11 Survivors Support Groups.

"Posttraumatic growth is a positive change experienced as a result of the struggle with a major life crisis or a traumatic event…We most definitely are not implying that traumatic events are good – they are not. But, for many of us, life crises are inevitable, and we are not given the choice between suffering and growth on the one hand, and no suffering and no change, on the other hand." (Source: https://ptgi.uncc.edu/what-is-ptg/)

Support Group Quotes

After returning home from New York and what I had gone through on 9/11, I had no one to talk to about what I had seen and what I was feeling. Luckily, a couple years later, and on the anniversary of 9/11, I was listening to the radio on my way into work and heard an interview with Joe Dittmar. I knew at that point I had to contact him and tell him who I was and what I went through.

A few days later, I met Joe and he told me about a group of 9/11 survivors from the Midwest that would meet and discuss their issues. This group would meet about once a month courtesy of Willow House and their unwavering support of 9/11 survivors.

Over the year that we met as a group, we talked about ourselves, we cried, and we laughed. Understanding everyone's stories gave me the ability to open up and share. Willow House was instrumental in giving me an outlet to express myself. I am forever grateful to Willow House for getting me through the most traumatic event in my lifetime.

Even though our group stopped meeting after a year, I made many friends that I continue to communicate with today. Many of those friends have contributed to this book.

Don Bacso

Through Willow House, I learned I was not alone. While I was surprised at how many World Trade Center Survivors there were in the greater Chicagoland area, it was impressive how well they were doing in facing challenges of PTSD, survivor's guilt, and trying to be normal in a post-normal world. In our sessions - which I later equated to our own little VFW-type group - listening fellow survivors share stories of the day, how they acted, what they did, what they witnessed, blew me away. As an Army officer, we are trained and prepared to operate in highly fluid, adverse conditions, and the demands 9/11 placed on the men and women - who were in New York on business was amazing.

We had many sessions where we would share, talk, listen, and support each other. The facilitators challenged and guided the discussions, ensuring we all had a voice and opportunities, and that we were in safety, a circle of friends. The challenges were to help us gain a sense of accountability, and to learn and grow, and not to wallow in grief or regret.

Ryan Yantis

We'd like to end our story with remarks Stefanie made at a 9/11 Memorial Service event in 2010, during which three trees were planted by Willow House at Northerly Island in Chicago, to honor and remember victims and to continue to help families and survivors heal.

"Gathering thoughts to write about Willow House's experience working with the bereaved families and survivors, one concept emerged repeatedly... the profound personal experiences on September 11th and thereafter, the grief and pain and courage of the families and survivors who lost their loved ones, friends and colleagues that day. That concept is REVERENCE.

There is a wonderful book I read soon after 9/11, entitled, *Reverence: Renewing a Forgotten Virtue*. Author Paul Woodruff defines reverence as "a developed capacity for inarticulate awe for what we recognize as transcending ourselves and our culture." Reverence, he said, is universal; it is an ancient virtue dating back thousands of years. It survives among us in half-forgotten patterns of behavior and in the vestiges of old ceremonies.

It is my hope for each of you to experience the peace and solace of reverence as we commemorate and observe September 11, 2001, in loving memory of those who lost their lives that day and in honor of the courage and humility of the survivors."

About Willow House

When I was a boy and I would see scary things in the news, my mother would say to me, "Look for the helpers. You will always find people who are helping."

-Fred Rogers

Willow House is a non-profit organization dedicated to developing and providing free supportive services for children, teens and young adults and their families coping with grief and the death of a parent, sibling or child. Willow House also provides education, training and consultation to the schools and communities seeking to support these families effectively. Based in the Chicagoland area since 1998, Willow House is known for its innovative programs, utilizing the latest research and best practices in mental health.

Willow House was founded on the following primary principles:

- Grief is a natural, normal response to a horrific, life-altering loss. It is not a "pathological condition;"
- Grief is uniquely personal. There is no timeline for grief, no stages of grief, no "right way" to grieve;
- No one should grieve alone.

For the most part, our culture is not well-equipped to provide the meaningful, honest, emotional and social support that is truly helpful and healing to grieving individuals. "It is too uncomfortable." Many "don't know what to say," and are afraid to mention or reference the deceased person by name, because "I don't want to make them cry." The exceptions to this are typically professionals and volunteers who are educated and experienced in providing grief support, while the most valuable support of others, are from those who "get it," because they are grieving themselves.

AMERICAN PRIDE INC.

ACKNOWLEDGEMENT

The Midwest, July 28, 2021

This book has been almost 20 years in the making, with our efforts starting in earnest almost a full year ago, in August 2020. The COVID-19 Pandemic and other factors allowed for a change in focus, and the situation aligned – along with great advisors, volunteers, and contributors – to make this possible.

Don Bacso and Ryan Yantis, under the American Pride Inc. banner, paved the way for our success thus far. Encouraged by those who have heard our speeches and presentations over the past several years, we had discussed the possibility of writing a book. It was always a good idea, but time and other realities (work, family, obligations, etc.) got in the way and it remained a "good idea". The "pause" caused by the pandemic provided the time and helped with the opportunity to make the "good idea" a reality.

Based on the results of a chance meeting in the summer of 2020 with Roxanne Boersma, a great young lady with a great deal of experience as a self-published author, we created a book proposal and outline, and made plans for the book. Weeks later in the fall of 2020, we engaged with Survivors from the World Trade Center and Pentagon and, received their support and commitment to share their stories. While not too onerous, this book has also been a challenge for many. During the writing process, one contributor messaged:

"This project has been emotionally and mentally draining, trying to remember 1 day and 3 months from 20 years ago."

We are grateful to all the Survivors who have shared their stories, had to think about and relive difficult times, and for any anxiety or discomfort they might have experienced. Our personal thanks to fellow the contributing Survivors - Laura Murphy, Bridget Pakowski, Trisha Shaffer Papantonakis, Joe Dittmar, Joe Chason, and Damon Wilkinson. In sharing your stories, you are making a positive difference and helping others to understand what it was like for you, on that day and since.

We understand that our stories are our memories of what we saw, experienced, and remember. We do not have a monopoly on the 9/11 Attacks, and others may have differing view or ideas. Hopefully, as evidenced by the personal accounts, we have all changed and grown from the events that day, and from surviving to share our stories. For some, this change has been profound, and others, more nuanced.

We also partnered with people who made a difference in service to others on 9/11, and in the days, weeks and months that followed. Nick Maviano was the Chicago-based "quarterback" who provided selfless service to others and helped connect stressed and terrified WTC Survivors with family and others in the immediate aftermath of the Attacks. Tom Van Cleave, a great Rotarian from Batavia, lived Rotary's motto of "service before self" in helping his business travelers that day, as well as taking care of a distraught mother seeking to honor her son. In sharing his story, Tom reminds us that there are reasons things happen, and wise people learn from others, and do not make similar mistakes.

There were many organizations and groups across the country who made a difference after 9/11, helping set things right and to help people heal. Two such organizations that made a huge difference for many of the Chicago area survivors were the

Union League Club of Chicago and Willow House. Willow House provided a focal point for many of the Survivors and gave us a time and place to be ourselves, with others who had shared the challenges and experiences on 9/11 in person. Thanks to Stefanie Norris, Kirsten Belzer, Denise O'Handley, and David Scheffler from Willow House for your efforts on this book, as well as for the great services Willow House provides to those dealing with grief and loss.

Ryan Yantis noted and prepared the ULCC's contributions from notes and memories he had, along with the observations and inputs from others. Ryan was a proud member of the club and appreciate their commitment to their core values of community, country, and culture. The ULCC made a difference for many of us, and we remain grateful.

Roxanne introduced us to an editor, who joined in as our volunteer editor. She, Roxanne, Don and Ryan formed the Editorial Team, and have spent considerable time editing, organizing, reordering, paginating, and preparing the book for release. We owe a great deal to Roxanne and our editor for their commitment to high standards and completing a professional manuscript for publication.

Thanks to an anonymous donor who prepared our very pleasing and eye-catching cover art as a volunteer, giving the finished product to American Pride for our use.

We are grateful to Coco Soodek, Attorney and owner of Seasongood Law, Inc. for her support, advice and counsel on matters relating to the book and our non-profit.

Gary Sinise has been an inspirational figure to many of us, first from his on-screen performances, and later by his dynamic, deep and personal engagement to help military, veterans, first responders and others, including our little group of Survivors.

We are grateful and appreciate his taking the time and effort to help us tell our story. A special hat-tip to Sharon Tyk, a dynamic person and presence, very engaged in veteran programs and efforts, who helped us tell our stories, and make key connections.

For our families, thanks, for all you are and do for us. We appreciate your patience, understanding, love and support in making this book, and our continued journey since 9/11, possible.

Last, we are truly grateful for the interest and support of the people who come to hear us talk about our 9/11 experience, and those who encouraged this book, in particular. While we are there talking and sharing, we also hope our audiences hear, reflected in our words and accounts, the brave, selfless and noble actions and deeds of others that we witnessed on 9/11. Without the brave men and women of EMS, fire, law enforcement, military and other first responders, the outcome of the 9/11 Attacks would have been vastly worse. Please remember to keep them in your hearts and prayers, while they risk all for the safety and security of others, our communities, and our country.

American Pride Inc. is a non-profit we formed in 2014, to give form to our efforts as witnesses and speakers about our 9/11 experiences. We have been growing slowly since we first started and have learned much along the way. We are exploring new and more dynamic means of helping first responders in preparing for future challenges with better technology. In the meantime, we will keep reminding our audiences the critical role our first responders played in saving people, keeping them alive, and doing the right things on 9/11/2001.

We hope you have gained something useful from our book and memories, that you will step up and make a positive difference in your community, support out first responders, and also continue to support American Pride, Inc.

Many mistakenly believe 9/11 Attack Survivors received some portion of the money from a Victim Compensation Fund. This is not so. Our lucky ticket was making it out of a bad situation alive and living to share our stories. In this book, all the contributors – the Survivors and others – have provided their stories, accounts, and memories to support American Pride Inc. None are being compensated for their work.

All proceeds from this book go to American Pride Inc. To learn more, please visit our website at: https://www.americanpride-inc.org

Thank You,
The Men and Women of American Pride

Made in the USA
Monee, IL
09 November 2023